Loving Like
JESUS

In a World That Hurts and Hates

by

pam gillaspie

Loving like Jesus in a World That Hurts and Hates

Dedicated to . . .

Jackie

Welcome to the family!

Acknowledgements

My deep thanks to the ladies in my Bible study who patiently walk through pilot classes bearing with me and enduring the process, believing that God will teach them through His Word! Thank you to my small group. You know who you are. God has strengthened me through your ministry in my life in ways I will never be able to explain or repay. I am humbled beyond words by your ministry and friendships. Thank you, as always, to my family—Dave, Katie, Brad, Jackie, Mom and Dad—you embody the truths that 1 Corinthians 13 teaches and bless me beyond measure. Finally, thank you to my co-workers at Precept, in particular Rick and Pete, who sharpen not only my writing but my thinking! I am grateful!

Loving Like
JESUS
In a World That Hurts and Hates

There is nothing quite like your favorite pair of jeans. You can dress them up, you can dress them down. You can work in them, play in them, shop in them . . . live in them. They always feel right. It is my hope that the structure of this Bible study will fit you like those jeans; that it will work with your life right now, right where you are whether you're new to this whole Bible thing or whether you've been studying the Book for years!

How is this even possible? Smoke and mirrors, perhaps? The new mercilessly thrown in the deep end? The experienced given pompoms and the job of simply cheering others on? None of the above.

Sweeter than Chocolate!® flexible studies are designed with options that will allow you to go as deep each week as you desire. If you're just starting out and feeling a little overwhelmed, stick with the main text and don't think a second thought about the sidebar assignments. If you're looking for a challenge, then take the sidebar prompts and go ahead and dig all the way to China! As you move along through the study, think of the sidebars and "Digging Deeper" boxes as that 2% of lycra that you find in certain jeans . . . the wiggle-room that will help them fit just right.

Beginners may find that they want to start adding in some of the optional assignments as they go along. Experts may find that when three children are throwing up for three days straight, foregoing those assignments for the week is the way to live wisely.

Life has a way of ebbing and flowing and this study is designed to ebb and flow right along with it!

Enjoy!

How to use this study

Sweeter than Chocolate!® studies meet you where you are and take you as far as you want to go.

1. WEEKLY STUDY: The main text guides you through the complete topic of study for the week.

2. FYI boxes: For Your Information boxes provide bite-sized material to shed additional light on the topic.

> **FYI:**
>
> **Reading Tip: Begin with prayer**
> You may have heard this a million times over and if this is a million and one, so be it. Whenever you read or study God's Word, first pray and ask His Spirit to be your Guide.

3. ONE STEP FURTHER and other sidebar boxes: Sidebar boxes give you the option to push yourself a little further. If you have extra time or are looking for an extra challenge, you can try one, all, or any number in between! These boxes give you the ultimate in flexibility.

> **ONE STEP FURTHER:**
>
> **Word Study: *torah*/law**
> The first of eight Hebrew key words we encounter for God's Word is *torah* translated "law." If you're up for a challenge this week, do a word study to learn what you can about *torah*. Run a concordance search and examine where the word *torah* appears in the Old Testament and see what you can learn from the contexts.
>
> If you decide to look for the word for "law" in the New Testament, you'll find that the primary Greek word is *nomos*.
>
> Be sure to see what Paul says about the law in Galatians 3 and what Jesus says in Matthew 5.

4. DIGGING DEEPER boxes: If you're looking to go further, Digging Deeper sections will help you sharpen your skills as you continue to mine the truths of Scripture for yourself.

> **Digging Deeper**
>
> **What else does God's Word say about counselors?**
>
> If you can, spend some time this week digging around for what God's Word says about counselors.
>
> Start by considering what you already know about counsel from the Word of God and see if you can actually show where these truths are in the Bible. Make sure that the Word actually says what you think it says.

Loving Like
JESUS
In a World that Hurts and Hates

Week One
Building Up in a World That Tears Down

Let all things be done for building up.
—1 Corinthians 14:26b

There is, perhaps, no greater question for today's Church than how we are to love in a world that hates. We know how to love people who love us—everyone does, but when we get at angles with others, or worse yet, when people actively hate both us and our Master, the loving business can get tough. Let's be honest here, Jesus' command to love our neighbors as ourselves is a tall order under favorable circumstances and next to unfathomable under common ones.

And so for the next eight weeks, we are going to learn to observe, interpret, and apply in our lives what God's Word—specifically 1 Corinthians 13—says about love. As we go, it is my prayer that you will not let facts get stuck above your neck, but that you'll learn God's truth and that He will use His Word to transform you more and more into the image of His Son . . . the One who is the perfect picture of love!

FYI:

If You're in a Class
Complete **Week One** together on your first day of class. This will be a great way to start getting to know one another and will help those who are newer to Bible study get their bearings.

Notes

PRESUPPOSITIONS: WHAT ARE YOU BRINGING ALONG?

How do you define "love"? What makes a person or behavior "loving"?

In what ways does our culture define "love"? How does this compare with your view?

If you disagree with the cultural definition(s), what struggle does this pose in your day-to-day life?

INDUCTIVE STUDY: LETTING GOD'S WORD SPEAK FOR ITSELF

While it's important to consider our current views as we study, we want to do that primarily so we can hold them up to the plumb line of God's perfect Word. We'll do this through a process called Inductive Bible Study which simply means that we'll be using the Bible itself as our primary resource.

This may sound simple and obvious, but an epidemic of biblical illiteracy is making this less and less common, even in the Church as people increasingly follow the views of people rather than taking the time to discover God's truth for themselves.

There are three basic components of Inductive Bible study: observation, interpretation, and application.

OBSERVATION

As we observe the text of Scripture, we read carefully and seek to answer the question: *What does the text say?* Slow and thoughtful reading is the core competency in observation and certain tools can help us in that.

- Asking 5 W and H questions — Who? What? When? Where? Why? and How?

- Identifying and marking **key words** — Key words are critical to understanding and typically repeated. When marking key words, you'll want to mark synonyms and pronouns, too.

- Making **Lists** — Key words are the basis for lists. After we identify a key word, listing everything we learn about it helps us to better grasp what the text says.

INTERPRETATION

Careful observation is invaluable as we begin to interpret the text and answer the question: *What does the text mean?* As we interpret, we're looking for one meaning. It's not uncommon for people to mix up interpretation and application. You've probably witnessed this when you've heard a person ask, "What does this verse mean *to you*?"

The text of Scripture does not change meaning based on who is reading it. It means what it means. As an author, I have a purpose in writing. You may think I'm trying to say something other than what I've said, but that does not change my meaning. It means you've misinterpreted. As people misinterpret human authors from time to time, they can also misinterpret the Divine One!

When we interpret, we observe the text closely and then look for the one meaning God intended. Here are some tools that will help immensely in discovering the text's meaning.

- Paying close attention to **context** — The context is simply the setting in which something dwells. In 1 Corinthians 13 we need to pay close attention to surrounding chapters.

- Checking **cross-references** — Cross-references are other places in Scripture that talk about the same topic.

- Allowing **Scripture to interpret Scripture** — The best commentary on Scripture is other Scripture. When we use cross-references we are allowing Scripture to interpret Scripture.

APPLICATION

Once we discover the meaning of the text, we can begin to apply it in our lives. Application needs to be anchored in the meaning of the text, but many and varied applications can come from one meaning. James, for example, talks about controlling the tongue in the third chapter of his letter. How that specifically applies in day-to-day life will probably be different in my life than yours, but it will be anchored in the same truth of honoring God through what we do and don't do. Bible study is never complete without application . . . and application starts at home. (And by "at home" I don't mean you apply the Word to your spouse and kids and then go after the neighbors! Application starts with *me!*)

The Goal: TRANSFORMATION!

If you're just the Bible rock star who can clobber all your friends in trivia, there's a big problem. The goal of inductive study is never knowledge for knowledge's sake, but rather understanding of God's Word that transforms lives.

Loving Like
JESUS
In a World that Hurts and Hates

Notes

What does the text say?

OBSERVATION . . . START BY LOOKING AT THE BIG PICTURE

We're going to read 1 Corinthians 13 over and over again, so relax and enjoy . . . the pressure is really off in this part, because we're just overviewing the passage looking for what is obvious and clear.

As we observe, we're going to **mark** a key repeated word and then we'll ask a couple of basic *Who? What? When? Where? Why?* and *How?* questions. Simple right?

READ 1 Corinthians 13 and **MARK** every occurrence of the repeated word *love*.

1 Corinthians 13

1 *If I speak with the tongues of men and of angels, but do not have love, I have become a noisy gong or a clanging cymbal.*

2 *If I have the gift of prophecy, and know all mysteries and all knowledge; and if I have all faith, so as to remove mountains, but do not have love, I am nothing.*

3 *And if I give all my possessions to feed the poor, and if I surrender my body to be burned, but do not have love, it profits me nothing.*

4 *Love is patient, love is kind and is not jealous; love does not brag and is not arrogant,*

5 *does not act unbecomingly; it does not seek its own, is not provoked, does not take into account a wrong suffered,*

6 *does not rejoice in unrighteousness, but rejoices with the truth;*

7 *bears all things, believes all things, hopes all things, endures all things.*

8 *Love never fails; but if there are gifts of prophecy, they will be done away; if there are tongues, they will cease; if there is knowledge, it will be done away.*

9 *For we know in part and we prophesy in part;*

10 *but when the perfect comes, the partial will be done away.*

11 *When I was a child, I used to speak like a child, think like a child, reason like a child; when I became a man, I did away with childish things.*

12 *For now we see in a mirror dimly, but then face to face; now I know in part, but then I will know fully just as I also have been fully known.*

13 *But now faith, hope, love, abide these three; but the greatest of these is love.*

FYI:

Start with Prayer

You've probably heard it before and if we study together again, you'll hear it again. Whenever you read or study God's Word, first ask His Spirit to be your Guide. Jesus says that the Spirit will lead us into all truth.

FYI:

Do I have to mark the text?

Of course not! But marking the text does help us see what is repeated and important. 1 Corinthians 13 is a perfect example of how marking the text will help you see the key word and how identifying the key word will help you identify the main topic or theme of a chapter or book. If you're colored-pencil phobic, no worries, you don't have to mark. If you're willing to give it a try, though, I think it's worth a shot!

Loving Like
JESUS
In a World that Hurts and Hates

DISCUSS with your GROUP or PONDER on your own . . .

Who is writing and who is he writing to? (You need some additional information from the letter to answer this. If you know it, write it down; if not, we'll get there.)

What is the chapter's main topic? How do you know? (Don't overthink this!)

Note each time you marked the key word *love* and make a simple list of everything the chapter teaches about it. (It'll probably be a pretty long list. Don't forget to mark the references, too.)

FYI:

Corinth . . . A Lot Like Us

The Apostle Paul wrote 1 Corinthians to a church in Corinth, a port city in Greece that had been rebuilt and colonized by Rome during the reign of Julius Caesar.

Corinth was a trade city where people had opportunity to break free from the typical class structure of the day.

In Paul's day, many Corinthians were pull-yourself-up-by-your-own-bootstraps rich while others languished in poverty. Those who succeeded typically did so with an entrepreneurial, me-first, whatever-it-takes-to-win approach and the Church too often reflected the culture around it.

Loving Like
JESUS
In a World that Hurts and Hates

Digging Deeper

Read and Summarize 1 Corinthians by Chapter

We'll be reading the immediate context of 1 Corinthians 13 together (yup, just turn the page!). The best way to get the full picture, though, is to read Paul's whole 16-chapter letter. If you have time this week, read or listen to 1 Corinthians to get the full context of the 13th chapter. It will take a bit of time, but time invested in God's Word is never wasted!

Ask the 5 W and H questions as you read, give a one sentence summary of each chapter . . . and #hashtag each with a one word theme or highlight.

1   #

2   #

3   #

4   #

5   #

6   #

7   #

8   #

9   #

10   #

11   #

12   #

13   #

14   #

15   #

16   #

Listening resources:
https://www.biblegateway.com/audio/mcconachie/nasb/1Cor.1 (FREE streaming)

https://itunes.apple.com/au/audiobook/1-2-corinthians-bible-experience/id401949013 ($5.99)

Loving Like
JESUS
In a World that Hurts and Hates

What does the text mean?

INTERPRETATION ... STARTING THE PROCESS

We'll be continually observing and interpreting as we walk through this study, all the while looking to apply what we're learning. As we begin the interpretation process, we need to start by exploring the context of 1 Corinthians 13. Many people assume 1 Corinthians 13 is about a generalized emotion, others view it as "the wedding passage," and still others see it as a deep well of inspirational quotations—greeting card heaven! The context, however, moves the interpretation of the chapter in a direction that is very different from these views. Let's check out this context, the neighborhood 1 Corinthians 13 lives in.

READ 1 Corinthians 12–14 in your Bible paying close attention to the topics being addressed in the chapters that sandwich our main text. You may want to look at the following questions before you begin reading.

DISCUSS with your GROUP or PONDER on your own . . .

1 CORINTHIANS 12
What do we know about Paul's readers from 1 Corinthians 12:1? Explain.

What is Paul's main topic in chapter 12? What is he concerned that his readers know about?

What example does he use to illustrate his point? How does he explain it?

In your own words, how do people fit together in the Church? What makes it possible?

ONE STEP FURTHER:

Word Study: Division

If you have some extra time this week, investigate the word translated "division" in 1 Corinthians 12:25. Begin by identifying the Greek word and then see how it is used throughout Paul's writings and the rest of the New Testament. Then record your findings below. As you do, consider whether what Paul is saying ever rears its head at your church. If it does, do you ever contribute to the problem? If so, how can you be part of the solution instead?

If you've never done a word study, there are step-by-step instructions for online word studies at the end of the lesson on page 15.

**Loving Like
JESUS**
In a World that Hurts and Hates

Week One: **Building Up in a World That Tears Down**

What problems can show up? Why?

What does Paul tell them to do in verse 31? Given just this chapter, do we know what the "greater gifts" are or do we need more information? Explain.

What is the "still more excellent way" Paul refers to in 1 Corinthians 12:31? What does that statement introduce?

How does 1 Corinthians 12 tie in to 1 Corinthians 13?

1 CORINTHIANS 14

How do the main points of 1 Corinthians 12 and 13 tie in with the first verse of 1 Corinthians 14? What does Paul say the Church should pursue? What should believers earnestly desire?

What two gifts does Paul specifically discuss in 1 Corinthians 14? Why do you think he mentions them?

Briefly explain 1 Corinthians 13's context.

OBSERVE the TEXT of SCRIPTURE

Before we move on, let's look a little closer at two portions of the texts we've just read.

READ 1 Corinthians 12:20-26 and **MARK** every occurrence of the repeated word *body*. Then, **MARK** every reference to *members* in a different way.

1 Corinthians 12:20-26

20 But now there are many members, but one body.

21 And the eye cannot say to the hand, "I have no need of you"; or again the head to the feet, "I have no need of you."

22 On the contrary, it is much truer that the members of the body which seem to be weaker are necessary;

23 and those members of the body which we deem less honorable, on these we bestow more abundant honor, and our less presentable members become much more presentable,

24 whereas our more presentable members have no need of it. But God has so composed the body, giving more abundant honor to that member which lacked,

25 so that there may be no division in the body, but that the members may have the same care for one another.

26 And if one member suffers, all the members suffer with it; if one member is honored, all the members rejoice with it.

> **INDUCTIVE FOCUS:**
>
> **Contrasts and Comparisons**
> As we continue to observe the text, another tool we can use is identifying and thinking through contrasts and comparisons.

DISCUSS with your GROUP or PONDER on your own . . .

What does Paul contrast in this section? What is the primary contrast?

Loving Like
JESUS
In a World that Hurts and Hates

How are the body and the members related to one another?

What different kinds of members are there? What is their relationship to one another?

According to verse 25, what should be entirely absent from the body? What would this do to a physical body?

Does the Church today tolerate division? If so, why do you think it does?

What should characterize the relationship of members of the body, again according to verses 25-26?

How does this line up with your reality?

What does suffering with someone entail?

What about rejoicing with someone who is honored? Do you think that is easier or harder? Why?

OBSERVE the TEXT of SCRIPTURE

READ 1 Corinthians 14:1-6, 12, 26 and **MARK** every form of the word *edify.*

1 Corinthians 14:1-6, 12, 26

1 *Pursue love, yet desire earnestly spiritual gifts, but especially that you may prophesy.*

2 *For one who speaks in a tongue does not speak to men but to God; for no one understands, but in his spirit he speaks mysteries.*

3 *But one who prophesies speaks to men for edification and exhortation and consolation.*

4 *One who speaks in a tongue edifies himself; but one who prophesies edifies the church.*

5 *Now I wish that you all spoke in tongues, but even more that you would prophesy; and greater is one who prophesies than one who speaks in tongues, unless he interprets, so that the church may receive edifying.*

6 *But now, brethren, if I come to you speaking in tongues, what will I profit you unless I speak to you either by way of revelation or of knowledge or of prophecy or of teaching?*

12 *So also you, since you are zealous of spiritual gifts, seek to abound for the edification of the church.*

26 *What is the outcome then, brethren? When you assemble, each one has a psalm, has a teaching, has a revelation, has a tongue, has an interpretation. Let all things be done for edification.*

ONE STEP FURTHER:

Word Study: One Another

If you have some extra time this week, see what the Bible has to say about literally "one anothers" (Greek: *allelon*). What does Paul say elsewhere in Corinthians? In his other writings? What does Jesus say? What do other New Testament writers have to say? Use extra paper if you need to and then summarize below the highlights of what you've discovered.

Loving Like
JESUS
In a World that Hurts and Hates

DISCUSS with your GROUP or PONDER on your own . . .

Look back at every place you marked *edify* and *edification* and then make a short list of everything this passage teaches.

What does Paul say about the one who prophesies? What does this gift produce according to verses 3 and 4?

How is pursuing love related to edifying others? Are these related in your life? If so how?

How often do you consider how your words or actions will build people up or tear them down before you speak or act? What effect does (or could!) considering this have on your life and the lives of those around you?

How do you think others in your life would answer the previous question with regard to you? Explain.

ONE STEP FURTHER:

Word Study: Pursue

If you have some extra time this week, investigate the word translated "pursue" in 1 Corinthians 14:1. Like other neutral Greek words, it acquires a positive or negative moral sense depending on what it's hooked up with; a person, for example, can pursue evil or righteousness. See if you can find where else it is used in the New Testament. Then explain how would you characterize the word? How is it usually translated when it is associated with something wrong? What else did you learn? Record your observations below.

FYI:

Edify

The English family of words edif* in 1 Corinthians 14 derive from the Greek verb *oikodomeo*, a compound of *oikos* (house) and *demo* (to build). In the Church, everything we do should be to the end of building the house, building the body, building *up*, not tearing *down*.

Loving Like
JESUS
In a World that Hurts and Hates

Digging Deeper

Where Else is Love?

Take some time to find and consider other examples of love in the Bible . . . . We'll be getting to them as we study, but it's more challenging and more fun to think through it on your own first! If the thought of this overwhelms you, move on. No worries, we'll hit the high points together. If it inspires you, though, get to it! Here are some broad categories to help you break this big task into smaller pieces.

The Books of the Law

Old Testament History Books

Old Testament Prophets

Old Testament Poetry/Wisdom Literature

New Testament Gospel Accounts

New Testament Historical Accounts

New Testament Letters

New Testament Apocalyptic Literature

Loving Like
JESUS
In a World that Hurts and Hates

@THE END OF THE DAY . . .

Take a little time to reflect on what you've studied this week. Without flipping back through the pages, what truth stood out to you the most? How is it changing how you are thinking and acting?

Now, go ahead and turn the pages and take some time to review where we've been. What truth most surprised you?

What truth did you most need to hear or be reminded of?

What is one way you can edify one of your "one another"s this week?

HOW TO DO AN ONLINE WORD STUDY

For use with www.blueletterbible.org

1. Type in Bible verse. Change the version to NASB. Click the "Search" button.

2. When you arrive at the next screen, you will see a button labeled "Tools" to the left of your verse.

   Hover over the "Tool" button and a list will pop up.

   Click the first button on the pop-up list—"Interlinear C"—to take you to the concordance link.

3. Click on the Strong's number which is the link to the original word in Greek or Hebrew.

Clicking this number will bring up another screen that will give you a brief definition of the word as well as list every occurrence of the Greek word in the New Testament or Hebrew word in the Old Testament. Before running to a dictionary definition, scan places where it's used in Scripture and examine the general contexts.

Week One: **Building Up in a World That Tears Down**

Week Two

Hidden Treasures

Your word I have treasured in my heart,
that I may not sin against You.
—Psalm 119:11

We've overviewed 1 Corinthians 13 and we've checked out the context. Hopefully you're starting to feel familiar with the text. This week, before we dive in headlong, we're going to circle back for a little bit to look at the authority and sufficiency of God's Word and the value of studying deeply enough to memorize the content. I know memorization is a tough sell. It takes the investment of time, which is a more valuable commodity than money. This is why it's critical for us to understand the reason and the value.

Don't let the idea of memorizing overwhelm you. Some of us will memorize all of 1 Corinthians 13, others a few verses, and still others may decide to commit key concepts to memory. Whatever the case, let's take some time to explore the *Why?* of hiding God's Word in our hearts!

Memorizing Scripture

OBSERVATION IN OVERDRIVE

We looked at the basics of Observation last week. To answer "What does the text say?" we're asking 5 W and H questions as we read, we're identifying key words, and then we're listing what we've learned.

As we begin to memorize this week, let's add a couple more observation tools that will help us see the text from several slightly different angles as we seek to learn everything we can and remember as much as possible.

The longer I study God's Word, the more convinced I become that memorizing is the best tool for inductive study and conversely that inductive study is the best way ever to memorize! When we memorize, we have to see how the text fits together and flows . . . and examining how the text fits and flows helps us remember what's going on.

Here are a few more **tips and tools** to use as we study:

• **Watch for patterns and repetitions.** While we've already been looking for key words, we also want to watch for repeated phrases. As we'll see next week in 1 Corinthians 13:1-3, Paul makes five "if I" statements and uses the phrase "but do not have love" three times. There is rhythm and pattern. When there is rhythm and pattern, everything becomes easier.

• **Identify comparisons and contrasts.** This is where we'll be camping today as we begin to commit verses 4-7 to memory. Paul talks in very specific terms about what love is and isn't, about what love does and doesn't.

• **Pay attention to time phrases.** What is now and what will happen later. What was when I was a child compared to what I am now as an adult.

• **Mark geographic locations if present.** No worries on this one in 1 Corinthians 13 but it's a big deal in other chapters.

• **Look for terms of conclusion.** When you see "thus," "therefore," "for this reason" or similar phrases, it's clear that the author is wrapping up or summarizing a thought. These phrases usually precede something notable.

OBSERVE the TEXT of SCRIPTURE

READ 2 Timothy 3:16-17 and **MARK** *Scripture*. Then **UNDERLINE** everything that describes what it is and what benefits it provides.

2 Timothy 3:16-17

16 *All Scripture is inspired by God and profitable for teaching, for reproof, for correction, for training in righteousness;*

17 *so that the man of God may be adequate, equipped for every good work.*

DISCUSS with your GROUP or PONDER on your own . . .

Make a simple list of everything you underlined about Scripture.

What two words does Paul use to describe Scripture? Why does each matter?

What are the specific ways Scripture is useful?

What will those who have been profited by Scripture "be" according to Paul?

Have these verses challenged or altered your view of the Bible? Have they strengthened it? Explain.

If you believe Scripture perfectly equips you to do what God has called you to do, how will this change how you think and act? Got any specifics to share?

ONE STEP FURTHER:

Word Study: Adequate

If you're thinking about doing one sidebar this week, do this one! See if you can find the Greek word translated "adequate" in 2 Timothy 3:17. Then, investigate how it is related to the word translated "equipped." If you have difficulty finding the Greek roots, check a few different English translations to see how else "adequate" is translated elsewhere. Record your findings below.

Loving Like
JESUS
In a World that Hurts and Hates

Notes

ONE STEP FURTHER:

Cross-Reference: "Meditates"

"Meditates" in Psalm 1:2 translates the Hebrew word *hagah*. If you have some extra time this week, take a look at some other places in Scripture this word shows up and record what you learn. Watch the context (it will be in parentheses) to get the big picture so you'll know the setting! With the psalms, go ahead and read each of the psalms the whole way through if you have time.

Joshua 1:8 (1:1-9)

Psalm 63:6

Psalm 71:24

Psalm 77:12

Psalm 143:5

OBSERVE the TEXT of SCRIPTURE

Paul tells us in 2 Timothy 3:16 that all Scripture is God-breathed and profitable. The psalmist shows some of the ways it profits him practically day to day and tells of his love for the Word of God and the God of the Word.

READ Psalm 1 and **MARK** the *blessed* and the *wicked* distinctively. Be sure to include synonyms.

Psalm 1

1 How blessed is the man who does not walk in the counsel of the wicked,

Nor stand in the path of sinners,

Nor sit in the seat of scoffers!

2 But his delight is in the law of the LORD,

And in His law he meditates day and night.

3 He will be like a tree firmly *planted by streams of water*,

Which yields its fruit in its season

And its leaf does not wither;

And in whatever he does, he prospers.

4 The wicked are not so,

But they are like chaff which the wind drives away.

5 Therefore the wicked will not stand in the judgment,

Nor sinners in the assembly of the righteous.

6 For the LORD knows the way of the righteous,

But the way of the wicked will perish.

DISCUSS with your GROUP or PONDER on your own . . .

What characterizes the blessed man? You may want to make a simple list of what he does, what he doesn't, and what he is.

How are the wicked described?

Loving Like JESUS
In a World that Hurts and Hates

What is the core difference between the two kinds of people?

What do you delight in?

Is there anything that you constantly think about day and night? Would you like to substitute God's Word for this particular thought?

Have you ever known a person who delights in God's Word and continually meditates on it? What did you make of it?

Why do you think many people do not? What barriers have kept you from delighting in and meditating on God's Word?

How can being firmly planted in God's Word benefit your life?

FYI:

Nothing More Efficient
Let's get gut-level practical here. We're *all* pressed for time. We're *all* pulled in a million directions by default unless we're taking radical steps to counteract it. Memorizing Scripture is one of the highest leverage practices available to you. Memorizing is something you can do *almost* anytime and anywhere but once you have Scripture memorized you can dwell on it *any*time, *any*where. You probably can't read and review while meditating on memorized scriptures (at least I can't) but every physical activity is compatible with it—waiting for the kids, walking the dog, doing laundry, trying to fall asleep. It's like the Dr. Seuss book *I Can Read with My Eyes Shut.* Oh, yeah!

Loving Like
JESUS
In a World that Hurts and Hates

Digging Deeper

Remember and Review

If you have time, sit down with a cup of coffee and think back over some of the Scripture you've memorized over your lifetime. If you came to Christ as an adult, you may not have any—that's not a problem. Just move on to the next page. It will still be encouraging for you to hear in class how God has used Scripture treasured in your classmates' hearts in their lives.

What are some verses you have memorized over the course of your life?

Why did you memorize? (Prizes? Threats? Be honest!)

What methods/practices have helped you memorize?

What verse/passage you've memorized has been the most significant in your life?

How has God used this scripture in your life? How would you encourage others in this discipline?

OBSERVE the TEXT of SCRIPTURE

READ Psalm 119:9-16 and **MARK** every synonym for the Word of God (*word, commandment, statute, ordinance, testimony, precept*). Then **MARK** every reference the psalmist makes to himself (*I, me, my*).

Psalm 119:9-16

9 *How can a young man keep his way pure?*

   By keeping it according to Your word.

10 *With all my heart I have sought You;*

   Do not let me wander from Your commandments.

11 *Your word I have treasured in my heart,*

   That I may not sin against You.

12 *Blessed are You, O LORD;*

   Teach me Your statutes.

13 *With my lips I have told of*

   All the ordinances of Your mouth.

14 *I have rejoiced in the way of Your testimonies,*

   As much as in all riches.

15 *I will meditate on Your precepts*

   And regard Your ways.

16 *I shall delight in Your statutes;*

   I shall not forget Your word.

DISCUSS with your GROUP or PONDER on your own . . .

What overriding concern does the psalmist address in this stanza? Why is it important to him? To us?

Looking at what you marked, what does the psalmist say about God's Word? (Remember, we're including synonyms.)

FYI:

Who is the Psalmist?

We don't know for sure who wrote Psalm 119, the 176-verse acrostic poem that leaves next to nothing unsaid about what God's Word is and does. If you threatened my family and my dog, though, I'd tell you that my opinion is David. The internal evidence tells of a man who saw the highest of highs and the lowest of lows, one who was on the radar of princes, who was hunted and spent much time on the run as others sought his life. While some scholars attribute the Psalm to Ezra the scribe, my money's on David . . . the shepherd, the king, the man after God's own heart.

FYI:

Want more Psalm 119?

Why stop with one stanza?! Study all 176 verses in-depth with *Sweeter than Chocolate!* ® Psalm 119 and discover for yourself the sweet words and real solutions for life it teaches!

Loving Like
JESUS
In a World that Hurts and Hates

ONE STEP FURTHER:

Cross-Reference: The Other "Meditate"

Another Hebrew word commonly translated "meditate" is *siyah* (Psalm 119:15). The basic meaning is to rehearse, think something over and over.* It is always associated with content. Biblical meditation is never about emptying the mind, but filling it with God's Word and reviewing it.

If you have time this week, search on *siyah* and see where and how it is used throughout the Old Testament . . . and whatever you do, don't miss Proverbs 6:22 (where it is translated "talk"). When you're done, record your observations below.

*Cohen, Gary G. "2255 siyah." Edited by R. Laird Harris, Gleason L. Archer Jr., and Bruce K. Waltke. *Theological Wordbook of the Old Testament.* Chicago: Moody Press, 1999.

Week Two: **Hidden Treasures**

What is the psalmist's relationship with God and His Word?

Looking specifically at the tenses of the verbs, will the psalmist ever "arrive"? Will he ever "have it" and not need to continually pursue God through His Word? Explain.

Human beings are not neutral creatures. Our hearts will seek *after something*. Our lips will speak *of something*. Our minds will meditate *on something*. The psalmist sought God and His Word . . . but I wonder, what do we seek? Think for a moment how you would answer the following questions:

- *What do I seek with all my heart?*

- *What do I wander after?*

- *What do I treasure in my heart?*

- *What do I talk to people about?*

- *What do I rejoice in?*

- *What do I think about all the time?*

- *What ways do I respect?*

- *What delights me?*

- *What is important enough to me to remember?*

As you seek to walk in God's way, do you think any alterations need to be made to your life with respect to the Word? If so, what?

How would you explain the importance of the Word to someone else?

FYI:

Tips for Memorizing
Did you know that a dry erase marker works on a mirror . . . without damaging it? A simple way to keep the Word in front of your face throughout the day is to literally keep it in front of your face! Put a verse on each mirror in the house until you have it memorized. The family may have fun with it, too! If nothing else, they'll help keep you accountable for what you're learning!

MEMORIZING THE GUTS

Next week we are going to go back to the beginning of 1 Corinthians 13 and journey verse by verse by verse through the chapter. We'll dig and cross-reference and be stunned (I hope and pray!) by the joy of discovery. Before we go there, though, we're going to start by beginning to memorize the guts of what love **is** and **isn't,** what it **does** and **doesn't.** We'll polish the words as we go; we won't begin perfectly but we're going to start!

As we study this week, you're probably going to wonder, "What exactly does that word mean?" or "How should we interpret this word?" That's okay; as a matter of fact that will be great! We'll answer those questions in due time. This week, though, we're going to look at basic content and patterns to find different ways to remember the truths we're taking in.

In a sense, we're going to reverse engineer the middle section of the text. Paul weaves all of love's characteristics into a tapestry. We're going to look at the pieces separately to understand each one and how they relate and then put them back together to see them as part of the greater whole.

As we do this, we'll be sure not to overlook anything. We won't gloss, we won't ignore. We'll deal. I'll deal with "love does not take into account a wrong suffered" . . . who knows what God will have you dealing with. Well, He knows!

Week Two: **Hidden Treasures**

OBSERVE the TEXT of SCRIPTURE

READ 1 Corinthians 13:4-8 and 13.

1 Corinthians 13:4-8, 13

4 *Love is patient, love is kind and is not jealous; love does not brag and is not arrogant,*

5 *does not act unbecomingly; it does not seek its own, is not provoked, does not take into account a wrong suffered,*

6 *does not rejoice in unrighteousness, but rejoices with the truth;*

7 *bears all things, believes all things, hopes all things, endures all things.*

8 *Love never fails; but if there are gifts of prophecy, they will be done away; if there are tongues, they will cease; if there is knowledge, it will be done away.*

13 *But now faith, hope, love, abide these three; but the greatest of these is love.*

DISCUSS with your GROUP or PONDER on your own . . .

Read the text again and **CIRCLE** everything love *is* then list it below.

Read the text again. This time **UNDERLINE** and list below everything love *isn't.*

Stick with me. Read the text again. This time **CIRCLE** everything love *does* and list it below.

Finally, read the text one more time and **UNDERLINE** what love *doesn't*. Again, list below what you've marked.

Paul gives us a three-dimensional, rich, multi-faceted look at love. Are you beginning to see it? What it does and doesn't do has everything to do with what it is . . . and isn't. Biblical love isn't about behavioral modification. It is about *new* hearts and *new* behaviors that match. So, now, let's piece together everything that we've just listed into a simple chart.

Love **IS**

Love **ISN'T**

Love **DOES**

Love **DOESN'T**

ONE STEP FURTHER:

Why not now?

Since this study is getting in my business, I'm thinking, why not yours, too. We're in this together, right?

Even without digging too deeply into the is/isn't and does/doesn't section of 1 Corinthians 13, you're probably already starting to be aware of some of the, well, rougher edges of your life. If you're up for it, go ahead and write down what you think is typically the most challenging aspect of love for you.

I'll even go first. "Love is not provoked" is kind of, well, provoking me. As I've been memorizing, I'm much more aware of when *I am provoked*. I'm typically a roll with the punches, easy-going girl, which makes me very aware when I'm not. In certain things, I'm finding, I am easily provoked. It doesn't stop there. When I'm provoked, I rarely strike back but I do keep score. Ouch! There's another one. Love doesn't keep score (that's my loose paraphrase of verse 5b). God is changing me, but I'm a work in progress!

Your turn.

Loving Like JESUS
In a World that Hurts and Hates

Digging Deeper

Matthew, Mark, or Luke . . . Your Pick!

If you have extra time this week, read or listen through one of the synoptic Gospels—Matthew, Mark, or Luke. As you do, pay attention to the way Jesus interacts with people and shows love in action.

How Jesus talked to people:

How Jesus treated people:

What I can learn:

WHY MEMORIZE *THIS* SCRIPTURE?

There are some things in Scripture that are tough to understand and explain. Take propitiation, for example. How exactly do you explain that one? I'll never forget trying to help my third grade AWANA kids understand that. Neither the definition nor the concept is simple.

What about the Trinity? Again, we attempt to define a concept that accords with all the relevant scriptures without contradiction, but we have to resort to complex terms like being, essence, and substance. So while the Trinity is not contradictory, it's also not simple. Similarly even the Apostle Peter, writing about the Apostle Paul, says that he writes some things that while not contradictory are "hard to understand" (2 Peter 3:16)!

But here in 1 Corinthians 13, as throughout the Bible, God repeatedly lays out love specifically and illustratively. We may still have a tough time applying this truth, but let's not miss the clear teaching of what love is and isn't, does and doesn't. There is no excuse for missing something that is unfolded with such specificity and clarity!

So when you're tempted to walk out because you "don't love him anymore," hold your thoughts and emotions up to the truth of what God says about love. When you decide the anger's okay because she provoked you, remember the truth that love isn't provoked. When you realize you keep score better than the IRS, it's time to let God's double-edged sword do its perfect work in your life.

Remember where we started today:

2 Timothy 3:16–17

16 *All Scripture is inspired by God and profitable for teaching, for reproof, for correction, for training in righteousness;*

17 *so that the man of God may be adequate, equipped for every good work.*

Scripture is God-breathed and profitable, but we can't live what we don't know!

@THE END OF THE DAY . . .

Thinking back through what we've learned this week about love, where are you the strongest? Where are you the weakest? What do you most need to learn? Remember, this is not your own battle to fight. We can love because God first loved us. He empowers us to live . . . and love!

Loving Like
JESUS
In a World that Hurts and Hates

Week Two: **Hidden Treasures**

Week Three
1 Corinthians 13:1-3: #Nothing

" . . . if I have all faith, so as to remove mountains,
but do not have love, I am nothing."
—1 Corinthians 13:2b

All and *nothing*, like *always* and *never*, are radical words so it's surprising to see Paul pull out the first two with regard to the spiritual gifts he is so concerned for the Corinthians to understand correctly. Remember the beginning of 1 Corinthians 12? Paul wants his readers to know about spiritual gifts and goes on to spend the better part of three chapters discussing the topic.

But as important as spiritual gifts are to the Church, Paul says that even if people have it all going for them in that arena—the tongues, the prophecies, the faith, the giving—without love it all adds up to a big Z.E.R.O., nada, nothing. Put another way, 3 pounds of mountain-moving faith x 0 pounds of love = 0 . . . and that, my friends, is sobering.

INDUCTIVE FOCUS:

Context Matters

We talked a bit about context when we started our study but now, having looked at Paul's discussion of spiritual gifts in 1 Corinthians 12, don't the opening verses of 1 Corinthians 13 make so much more sense?

When people fail to pay attention to context, they run an enormous risk of misinterpreting the Bible. Sometimes that leads to bad personal application. Other times it leads to, as my Pastor Josh would say, "weaponizing Scripture." Let's face it, with a book as big as the Bible, you can make private cases for all sorts of personal things out of context.

Context is a gift that keeps us from turning God's solid truth into fiction that suits our fancy.

REMEMBERING

Take a few minutes to summarize what you learned last week.

1 Corinthians 13:1-3

OBSERVE the TEXT of SCRIPTURE

READ 1 Corinthians 13:1-3 and **MARK** every reference to *love*. Also **MARK** every spiritual gift that you notice. Finally, **UNDERLINE** every "if" clause.

1 Corinthians 13:1-3

1   If I speak with the tongues of men and of angels, but do not have love, I have become a noisy gong or a clanging cymbal.

2   If I have the gift of *prophecy*, and know all mysteries and all knowledge; and if I have all faith, so as to remove mountains, but do not have love, I am nothing.

3   And if I give all my possessions to feed the poor, and if I surrender my body to be burned, but do not have love, it profits me nothing.

DISCUSS with your GROUP or PONDER on your own . . .

List the five "If" statements you underlined. Then, next to each, list the outcome when love is absent.

What commonalities do you notice among all five "If" statements? Standing alone, do they strike you as positive, negative, or neutral? Why?

What lack do these three verses focus on? How significant is it? How does it relate to even abundant spiritual gifts?

A LITTLE MORE ON SPIRITUAL GIFTS

Before we continue exegeting (the fifty-cent word for drawing meaning out) 1 Corinthians 13:1-3, let's take a little more time to look at three other passages in the New Testament on the topic of spiritual gifts with a particular focus on how they relate to love.

We've already read what Paul wrote to the Corinthians. Let's see what he wrote about spiritual gifts and love to the churches at Rome and Ephesus. We'll also look at what Peter had to say!

OBSERVE the TEXT of SCRIPTURE

READ Romans 12 and **MARK** every reference to *love*. Also **MARK** every reference to specific spiritual gifts you notice. Then **UNDERLINE** everything that describes how *love* behaves.

Romans 12

1   *Therefore I urge you, brethren, by the mercies of God, to present your bodies a living and holy sacrifice, acceptable to God,* which is *your spiritual service of worship.*

2   *And do not be conformed to this world, but be transformed by the renewing of your mind, so that you may prove what the will of God is, that which is good and acceptable and perfect.*

3   *For through the grace given to me I say to everyone among you not to think more highly of himself than he ought to think; but to think so as to have sound judgment, as God has allotted to each a measure of faith.*

4   *For just as we have many members in one body and all the members do not have the same function,*

5   *so we, who are many, are one body in Christ, and individually members one of another.*

6   *Since we have gifts that differ according to the grace given to us,* each of us is to exercise them accordingly: *if prophecy, according to the proportion of his faith;*

7   *if service, in his serving; or he who teaches, in his teaching;*

8   *or he who exhorts, in his exhortation; he who gives, with liberality; he who leads, with diligence; he who shows mercy, with cheerfulness.*

9   *Let* love *be without hypocrisy. Abhor what is evil; cling to what is good.*

10 *Be devoted to one another in brotherly love; give preference to one another in honor;*

11 *not lagging behind in diligence, fervent in spirit, serving the Lord;*

12 *rejoicing in hope, persevering in tribulation, devoted to prayer,*

13 *contributing to the needs of the saints, practicing hospitality.*

14 *Bless those who persecute you; bless and do not curse.*

15 *Rejoice with those who rejoice, and weep with those who weep.*

FYI:

Spiritual Gifts Passages
The Bible talks extensively about spiritual gifts in four passages:

• Romans 12
• 1 Corinthians 12
• Ephesians 4
• 1 Peter 4

Don't you love the repetitions of 12s and 4s so they're easier to remember?! I sure do!

Loving Like
JESUS
In a World that Hurts and Hates

16 *Be of the same mind toward one another; do not be haughty in mind, but associate with the lowly. Do not be wise in your own estimation.*

17 *Never pay back evil for evil to anyone. Respect what is right in the sight of all men.*

18 *If possible, so far as it depends on you, be at peace with all men.*

19 *Never take your own revenge, beloved, but leave room for the wrath of God, for it is written, "VENGEANCE IS MINE, I WILL REPAY," says the Lord.*

20 *"BUT IF YOUR ENEMY IS HUNGRY, FEED HIM, AND IF HE IS THIRSTY, GIVE HIM A DRINK; FOR IN SO DOING YOU WILL HEAP BURNING COALS ON HIS HEAD."*

21 *Do not be overcome by evil, but overcome evil with good.*

DISCUSS with your GROUP or PONDER on your own . . .

How do Paul's descriptions of spiritual gifts in Romans 12 and 1 Corinthians 12 compare with one another?

If Christians are all different members of one body as Paul describes, what happens when a part decides not to participate because it thinks it's inferior to another part? What happens when a part starts thinking it doesn't need the other parts?

What specific gifts does Paul mention in Romans 12:6-8? What operating instructions does he give?

What does Paul say about love in Romans 12:9? How have you observed this in the lives of others around you? What are some ways you're growing in applying this to yourself?

ONE STEP FURTHER:

Word Study: Hypocrisy

If you have some extra time this week, see what you can discover about the Greek word translated "without hypocrisy" (Greek: *anupokritos*). Where does Paul use the word? Where is it used in the New Testament? How is it translated? Record your findings below.

Loving Like
JESUS
In a World that Hurts and Hates

If our love is not genuine, what bad outcomes can we reasonably expect?

So, any bad outcome you'd like to share? How did you end up in the situation?

ONE STEP FURTHER:

Words for Love

If you have some extra time this week, see if you can discover the different Greek words translated "love" in the New Testament. Record them below along with anything else you observe about them based on their usage and context.

According to Romans 12 what are some ways we can display love towards believers?

What about towards unbelievers?

Do you think it is ever biblical for a believer to be combative? Why/why not? Defend your answer from Scripture (here and elsewhere).

Not to beat a horse, but how practically can people live according to the commands Paul has set out? Explain.

Loving Like
JESUS
In a World that Hurts and Hates

FYI:

Jesus Quotes Isaiah

"And He said to them, "Rightly did Isaiah prophesy of you hypocrites, as it is written:

'THIS PEOPLE HONORS ME WITH THEIR LIPS,

BUT THEIR HEART IS FAR AWAY FROM ME.

'BUT IN VAIN DO THEY WORSHIP ME,

TEACHING AS DOCTRINES THE PRECEPTS OF MEN.'

"Neglecting the commandment of God, you hold to the tradition of men."
　　　　　　　—Jesus, Mark 7:6-8

Week Three: **1 Corinthians 13:1-3: #Nothing**

Digging Deeper

Hypocrites

Jesus had compassion on those who found it hard to follow, He saved a woman caught in the act of adultery—*in the act*—from stoning, He was kind and gentle with sinners of so many different stripes. Hypocrites, though, He called out because they only pretended to follow God. Take some time to see what Jesus has to say about them in Matthew 23.

Describe the setting of Matthew 23.

How does Jesus describe the scribes and Pharisees in Matthew 23:1-12?

What statements does he make about them in Matthew 23:13-39?

Give an example of when and where you were hypocritical. What made you aware of it?

What can we learn from Jesus' words in this chapter?

OBSERVE the TEXT of SCRIPTURE

READ Ephesians 4:11-16 and **MARK** every reference to *love*. Also **MARK** every reference to growing up (*mature, no longer to be children, grow up, growth,* etc.) Finally, read the text one more time and **MARK** every reference to the first person plural pronoun *we*.

Ephesians 4:11-16

11 And He gave some as apostles, and some as prophets, and some as evangelists, and some as pastors and teachers,

12 for the equipping of the saints for the work of service, to the building up of the body of Christ;

13 until we all attain to the unity of the faith, and of the knowledge of the Son of God, to a mature man, to the measure of the stature which belongs to the fullness of Christ.

14 As a result, we are no longer to be children, tossed here and there by waves and carried about by every wind of doctrine, by the trickery of men, by craftiness in deceitful scheming;

15 but speaking the truth in love, we are to grow up in all aspects into Him who is the head, even Christ,

16 from whom the whole body, being fitted and held together by what every joint supplies, according to the proper working of each individual part, causes the growth of the body for the building up of itself in love.

DISCUSS with your GROUP or PONDER on your own . . .

What gifts does Paul mention in verse 11? What are they given for?

What is the endgame of the gifts, the long-term goal?

What does Paul say with regard to building up and growing up? Make a short list based on what you marked.

Loving Like
JESUS
In a World that Hurts and Hates

Week Three: **1 Corinthians 13:1-3: #Nothing**

What characteristic makes children vulnerable to danger? What specific dangers do they face and what's common among them?

FYI:

Deceived by Craftiness

But I am afraid that, as the serpent deceived Eve by his craftiness, your minds will be led astray from the simplicity and purity of devotion *to Christ.*

—2 Corinthians 11:3

What winds of doctrine have you noticed blowing around? Trickeries? Schemes?

What did you learn about the body of Christ by marking the word *we*? Make a short list.

Who needs to "grow up"?

So, not to get too personal here, but if you feel like you're reasonably "grown up" in the faith, are you off the hook according to Ephesians? Explain.

How are we to help one another grow up? What do you think *your* role is, given where you are in your spiritual development?

Loving Like
JESUS

In a World that Hurts and Hates

Digging Deeper

The Gospel of John

As we did last week with the Synoptic Gospels, this week read (or listen) and pay attention to the way Jesus interacts with people and shows love in action in the Gospel of John.

How Jesus talked to people:

How Jesus treated people:

What I can learn:

Loving Like
JESUS
In a World that Hurts and Hates

Week Three: **1 Corinthians 13:1-3: #Nothing**

OBSERVE the TEXT of SCRIPTURE

READ 1 Peter 4:7-11 and **MARK** every reference to *love* and to *one another*.

1 Peter 4:7-11

7 *The end of all things is near; therefore, be of sound judgment and sober spirit for the purpose of prayer.*

8 *Above all, keep fervent in your love for one another, because love covers a multitude of sins.*

9 *Be hospitable to one another without complaint.*

10 *As each one has received a special gift, employ it in serving one another as good stewards of the manifold grace of God.*

11 *Whoever speaks, is to do so as one who is speaking the utterances of God; whoever serves is to do so as one who is serving by the strength which God supplies; so that in all things God may be glorified through Jesus Christ, to whom belongs the glory and dominion forever and ever. Amen.*

DISCUSS with your GROUP or PONDER on your own . . .

What time phrase does Peter use in verse 7? What term of conclusion? What do these have to do with his two commands to his readers?

What does he say is most important in verse 8?

Who are the "one another"s in this passage? What are we supposed to do for and to them?

ONE STEP FURTHER:

Keep Fervent

To help you understand the intensity of what Peter is telling his readers to do, check out the following verses and observe how words related to the Greek root *teino* are used.

Luke 22:44

Luke 23:10

Acts 7:55

Acts 12:5

1 Peter 1:22

Loving Like
JESUS
In a World that Hurts and Hates

How would you describe your love for the brethren? Your attitude in serving?

How do you think your "one another"s would describe your love? (Sorry, this is always a clarifying question for me.)

Again, what is the power behind all of this—the love, the speaking and the serving gifts? Not to belabor the point, but what will eventually happen if you try to power your own engine?

ONE STEP FURTHER:

Love Covers Sins?
Okay, isn't it Jesus' blood that covers sins? If our love can cover sins we don't need a Savior, right? Is Peter, then, referring to something else? Take some time this week to study the passage more closely to see what Peter says, what he means, and how it applies. Once you've answered the question on your own, compare with a commentary or two to check your work. Record your findings below.

1 Corinthians 13:1-3
OBSERVE the TEXT of SCRIPTURE

As we return to 1 Corinthians 13:1-3, let's compare it with a passage that sheds light on a person who behaves in a way that looks good without being good, that appears loving but actually has ulterior motives. Remember as you read, Romans 12:9 tells us that love is to be without hypocrisy.

READ 1 Corinthians 13:1-3 and **MARK** the phrase *but do not have love.*

1 Corinthians 13:1-3

1 *If I speak with the tongues of men and of angels, but do not have love, I have become a noisy gong or a clanging cymbal.*

2 *If I have the gift of prophecy, and know all mysteries and all knowledge; and if I have all faith, so as to remove mountains, but do not have love, I am nothing.*

3 *And if I give all my possessions to feed the poor, and if I surrender my body to be burned, but do not have love, it profits me nothing.*

**Loving Like
JESUS**
In a World that Hurts and Hates

Week Three: **1 Corinthians 13:1-3: #Nothing**

Now **READ** Matthew 6:1-8. As you read, **MARK** every references to *hypocrites*.

Matthew 6:1-8

1 *"Beware of practicing your righteousness before men to be noticed by them; otherwise you have no reward with your Father who is in heaven.*

2 *"So when you give to the poor, do not sound a trumpet before you, as the hypocrites do in the synagogues and in the streets, so that they may be honored by men. Truly I say to you, they have their reward in full.*

3 *"But when you give to the poor, do not let your left hand know what your right hand is doing,*

4 *so that your giving will be in secret; and your Father who sees what is done in secret will reward you.*

5 *"When you pray, you are not to be like the hypocrites; for they love to stand and pray in the synagogues and on the street corners so that they may be seen by men. Truly I say to you, they have their reward in full.*

6 *"But you, when you pray, go into your inner room, close your door and pray to your Father who is in secret, and your Father who sees what is done in secret will reward you.*

7 *"And when you are praying, do not use meaningless repetition as the Gentiles do, for they suppose that they will be heard for their many words.*

8 *"So do not be like them; for your Father knows what you need before you ask Him.*

DISCUSS with your GROUP or PONDER on your own . . .

What do the people referred to in 1 Corinthians 13:1-3 have and do? How do they compare with those in Matthew 6:1-8? Be sure to include contrast since the comparison is not always apple-to-apple.

What does each person look like externally? What does each lack?

What reward(s) do the people in Matthew 6:1-8 get? What reward(s) could they have had?

ONE STEP FURTHER:

Prophecy Gone Bad

For a couple of instances of prophets gone bad, check out the accounts of Balaam and Jonah.

God always accomplishes what He sets out to do but sometimes in spite of tools He uses. Balaam's account can be found in Numbers 22–24 with commentary on him in the New Testament accounts in 2 Peter 2:15, Jude 11, and Revelation 2:14.

You can find the life and times of Jonah in the Old Testament book named after him.

FYI:

What Does Profit!

Giving your body to be burned apart from love may not profit (Greek: *opheleo*) you a lick, but what never fails to profit those who hear with faith is God's Word . . . it is "living and active and sharper than any two-edged sword" (Hebrews 4:12); it is God-breathed and profitable to make God's people perfectly suited to God's work (see 2 Timothy 3:16-17).

Let's get practical here. If the fanciest gift the Corinthians could come up with (although Paul disagreed with their assessment) was counted as noise without love, what about you and I simply speaking devoid of love? Think back over the past week. Have you indulged in gonging and clanging? If so, did you like the sound?

While the Corinthians wanted to speak in tongues, the gift that Paul valued much more highly was prophecy. Even if he had the gifts of prophecy, all knowledge, and mountain-moving faith, what did he say he would be without love? Does this change your view on the importance of love at all? If so, how?

Does Paul's emphasis on love mean that prophecy, knowledge, and faith are unimportant? How would you respond to someone who says none of the gifts are important; all you need is love? Be sure to answer from the Word and cite your references.

Finally, what does Paul say about giving our possessions and selves apart from love? How does this compare with Matthew 6?

How would you summarize Paul's teaching in 1 Corinthians 13:1-3?

FYI:

Mountain-Moving Faith

" . . . for truly I say to you, if you have faith the size of a mustard seed, you will say to this mountain, 'Move from here to there,' and it will move; and nothing will be impossible to you.' "

—Jesus, Matthew 17:20

Loving Like
JESUS
In a World that Hurts and Hates

Week Three: **1 Corinthians 13:1-3: #Nothing**

Do you know what your spiritual gifts are? If so, jot them down. How do you go about operating your gifts in love?

One way to check to see if we are operating our gifts in love is to hold them up against the plumbline of Scripture. Let's see if you can remember from last week what we learned about what love *is* and *isn't,* what love *does* and *doesn't*. If you need to peek, go ahead, but try to see what you can do from memory first.

Love IS

Love ISN'T

Love DOES

Love DOESN'T

@THE END OF THE DAY . . .

It's tempting to think that gifting is valuable regardless of love but God's Word says that simply is not true. You may be wildly gifted, I may be the same . . . but if we don't have love, it all amounts to nothing.

Before you put your pencil down, reflect on what we've studied this week in God's Word and jot down whatever it is that you most need to remember.

Loving Like
JESUS
In a World that Hurts and Hates

Week Four

Love Is . . .

Love is patient, love is kind . . .
—1 Corinthians 13:4a

Is there anything more stressful than trying to manufacture patience when your insides are agitated with restlessness or trying to whip up a batch of kindness when the only ingredients on the shelf that day are "ticked off" and "annoyed"? You've probably been there. I know I have.

Paul doesn't allow for the excuse of circumstances when he leads his "love list" with two words that pack dramatic punch, *patient* and *kind,* both words steeped in who God, Himself, is. In them we see such simplicity and yet depth beyond both measure and comprehension. Let's get started.

Week Four: **Love Is . . .**

REMEMBERING

Take a few minutes to think back over what we've studied so far. Be sure to include both *what you've been learning* and *how you've been applying* what you've learned.

LET'S REVIEW . . .
1 Corinthians 13:1-3
OBSERVE the TEXT of SCRIPTURE

1 Corinthians 13:1-3

1 *If I speak with the tongues of men and of angels, but do not have love, I have become a noisy gong or a clanging cymbal.*

2 *If I have the gift of prophecy, and know all mysteries and all knowledge; and if I have all faith, so as to remove mountains, but do not have love, I am nothing.*

3 *And if I give all my possessions to feed the poor, and if I surrender my body to be burned, but do not have love, it profits me nothing.*

DISCUSS with your GROUP or PONDER on your own . . .

According to the text, what are you without love? What is the most crazily gifted person you know without love?

How has this truth been changing how you think and act?

1 Corinthians 13:4-7
OBSERVE the TEXT of SCRIPTURE

1 Corinthians 13:4-7

4 *Love is patient, love is kind and is not jealous; love does not brag and is not arrogant,*

5 *does not act unbecomingly; it does not seek its own, is not provoked, does not take into account a wrong suffered,*

6 *does not rejoice in unrighteousness, but rejoices with the truth;*

7 *bears all things, believes all things, hopes all things, endures all things.*

DISCUSS with your GROUP or PONDER on your own . . .

What does Paul say love "is"?

What initially comes to mind when you think of the words "patient" and "kind?" (Let's get these thoughts down so we can compare them with what we learn as we study!)

Although "patient" and "kind" are adjectives in English, find out what they are in Greek. (If you're not sure how to do this, refer to the end of the chapter for more info!) What do you make of this and the relationship of these two to love?

FYI:

Word Study: *Makrothumeo*
The word we read as "patient" in both the ESV and NASB translations of 1 Corinthians 13:4 comes from the Greek *makrothumeo*, a compound word that combines *makros* (long) and *thumos* (wrath or anger). If you have some extra time this week, explore how and where it is used by Paul and elsewhere in the New Testament. If you're really up for a challenge see if you can find where it is used in the *LXX* (the Greek translation of the Old Testament) and what Hebrew word(s) it typically corresponds to. Then record your findings below.

Loving Like
JESUS
In a World that Hurts and Hates

49

WHAT LOVE IS . . .

This week we're looking primarily at two words: patient (Greek: *makrothumeo*) and kind (Greek: *chresteuomai*). While they're translated as adjectives in English, they actually lead off a series of 15 verbs in 1 Corinthians 13:4ff that Paul uses to teach us about love.

As we examine *makrothumeo* and *chresteuomai*, we'll traverse the pages of Scripture starting by looking at God's description of Himself that includes, you guessed it, patience.

Perhaps you've noticed certain words in the language that we've gelded by overuse and misuse. Patience may top that list. If you think you've earned your "patience" badge because you can wait in line and not freak out when the Internet connection goes down, you may be surprised at what you discover!

As we do our cross-referencing, we'll pay attention as God Himself shows us through His Word how He defines patience and kindness.

OBSERVE the TEXT of SCRIPTURE

As Exodus 34 opens up Moses has been to the mountaintop and back in more ways than one! After receiving the tablets of the Law written by the hand of God and breaking them because of the golden calf incident, Moses asks God to show him His glory. We often try to describe God, but in the following verses *God describes Himself!*

READ Exodus 34:1-7 and **MARK** every reference to the *LORD*. Then **UNDERLINE** every word or phrase He uses to describe Himself.

Exodus 34:1-7

1 Now the LORD said to Moses, "Cut out for yourself two stone tablets like the former ones, and I will write on the tablets the words that were on the former tablets which you shattered.

2 "So be ready by morning, and come up in the morning to Mount Sinai, and present yourself there to Me on the top of the mountain.

3 "No man is to come up with you, nor let any man be seen anywhere on the mountain; even the flocks and the herds may not graze in front of that mountain."

4 So he cut out two stone tablets like the former ones, and Moses rose up early in the morning and went up to Mount Sinai, as the LORD had commanded him, and he took two stone tablets in his hand.

5 The LORD descended in the cloud and stood there with him as he called upon the name of the LORD.

6 Then the LORD passed by in front of him and proclaimed, "The LORD, the LORD God, compassionate and gracious, slow to anger, and abounding in lovingkindness and truth;

ONE STEP FURTHER:

God Describes Himself

If you have some extra time this week, get the whole context for God's self-description in Exodus 34:1-7 by reading Exodus 32–34 and record your observations below. Don't forget to ask the 5Ws and H as you go!

7   *who keeps lovingkindness for thousands, who forgives iniquity, transgression and sin; yet He will by no means leave the guilty unpunished, visiting the iniquity of fathers on the children and on the grandchildren to the third and fourth generations."*

DISCUSS with your GROUP or PONDER on your own . . .

Describe the setting. Where is Moses? Where are the other people? What does God do for Moses?

How does God describe Himself?

"Slow to anger" is the phrase that matches up with "patient" in 1 Corinthians 13. If God is "slow to anger" and yet "does not leave the guilty unpunished," how can these truths help grow your patience?

OBSERVE the TEXT of SCRIPTURE

God's description of Himself was not lost on the prophet Jonah who didn't want to deliver His message to the wicked and brutal people of Ninevah. We'll pick up the account after Jonah has proclaimed the coming judgment and the people have repented in sackcloth and ashes.

READ Jonah 3:10–4:11 and **MARK** every reference to *anger* (be sure to include *slow to anger*) and *compassion.*

Jonah 3:10–4:11

10   *When God saw their deeds, that they turned from their wicked way, then God relented concerning the calamity which He had declared He would bring upon them. And He did not do it.*

4:1   *But it greatly displeased Jonah and he became angry.*

FYI:

The Capital of Assyria

Before you're too hard on Jonah, realize that the people he was sent to pronounce judgment on were thieves and murderers. Nineveh was one of the capital cities of the Assyrian Empire and had a notorious reputation. If you've ever wished that terrorists would "get what's coming to them," you have more in common with Jonah than you may have thought. Something to consider.

Loving Like
JESUS
In a World that Hurts and Hates

Notes

ONE STEP FURTHER:

Psalms and the Attributes of God

If you have some time this week, check out the following references where the psalmist—like Jonah—refers to God's attributes using the same words we observed in Exodus 34:6-7. Check out the contexts and record what you learn below.

Psalm 86:15

Psalm 103:8

Psalm 145:8

2   He prayed to the LORD and said, "Please LORD, was not this what I said while I was still in my own country? Therefore in order to forestall this I fled to Tarshish, for I knew that You are a gracious and compassionate God, slow to anger and abundant in lovingkindness, and one who relents concerning calamity.

3   "Therefore now, O LORD, please take my life from me, for death is better to me than life."

4   The LORD said, "Do you have good reason to be angry?"

5   Then Jonah went out from the city and sat east of it. There he made a shelter for himself and sat under it in the shade until he could see what would happen in the city.

6   So the LORD God appointed a plant and it grew up over Jonah to be a shade over his head to deliver him from his discomfort. And Jonah was extremely happy about the plant.

7   But God appointed a worm when dawn came the next day and it attacked the plant and it withered.

8   When the sun came up God appointed a scorching east wind, and the sun beat down on Jonah's head so that he became faint and begged with all his soul to die, saying, "Death is better to me than life."

9   Then God said to Jonah, "Do you have good reason to be angry about the plant?" And he said, "I have good reason to be angry, even to death."

10   Then the LORD said, "You had compassion on the plant for which you did not work and which you did not cause to grow, which came up overnight and perished overnight.

11   "Should I not have compassion on Nineveh, the great city in which there are more than 120,000 persons who do not know the difference between their right and left hand, as well as many animals?"

DISCUSS with your GROUP or PONDER on your own . . .

How does God's revelation of Himself to Jonah compare with His revelation of Himself to Moses?

What attributes of God correspond with His actions toward the Ninevites?

What different things anger Jonah in this short section of text? Why does he become angry?

How does Jonah's attitude differ from that of the God he serves?

Have you had a Jonah moment, become angry with God because He held back what you considered to be a "right" judgment? If so, what can you learn and apply?

MORE *MAKROTHUMEO*

Both apostles Peter and Paul show concrete examples of how *makrothumeo* is bound up in God's saving work. Peter talks about it specifically with reference to the time of Noah, Paul in recounting his own life story!

OBSERVE the TEXT of SCRIPTURE

There are some tough interpretive issues in the following verses that are way beyond the scope of this study. Fortunately, the answers to these question won't change the way we interpret the portion of the text that has to do with the patience of God.

READ 1 Peter 3:18-20 and **MARK** *patience* and every reference to *God*.

1 Peter 3:18-20

18 *For Christ also died for sins once for all, the just for the unjust, so that He might bring us to God, having been put to death in the flesh, but made alive in the spirit;*

19 *in which also He went and made proclamation to the spirits now in prison,*

20 *who once were disobedient, when the patience of God kept waiting in the days of Noah, during the construction of the ark, in which a few, that is, eight persons, were brought safely through the water.*

INDUCTIVE PRINCIPLE:

Unclear in Light of the Clear

Most of the Bible is clear. "Children, obey your parents in the Lord, for this is right" (Ephesians 6:1) is not rocket science. Most of our trouble with the Bible is not understanding what it says, but making time to learn it in the first place and then taking care to act on what we know. From time to time, though, we run across passages that talk about things like Jesus making "proclamation to the spirits now in prison." Men and women far smarter than I don't agree on what 1 Peter 3:19 means. That doesn't mean we throw up our arms in despair. It means that from time to time, history and culture block us from being able to say definitively what a text means. When we encounter one of these texts we interpret it to the best of our ability in light of what is clear in the Scripture. Always, always, always we interpret the unclear in light of the clear and not the other way around.

Loving Like
JESUS
In a World that Hurts and Hates

DISCUSS with your GROUP or PONDER on your own . . .

According to the text, what did Christ do for us? What did that involve?

List everything the text tells us about God.

What biblical event does Peter point to as an example of God's patience?

OBSERVE the TEXT of SCRIPTURE

Remember that Scripture interprets Scripture. Peter says that God displayed His patience during the days of Noah. Let's take a look at that!

READ Genesis 5:32, 6:5-22 and 7:5-6. **MARK** time references. Also **MARK** every reference to *wickedness*, *corruption*, and *violence*.

Genesis 5:32

32 Noah was five hundred years old, and Noah became the father of Shem, Ham, and Japheth.

Genesis 6:5-22

5 Then the LORD saw that the wickedness of man was great on the earth, and that every intent of the thoughts of his heart was only evil continually.

6 The LORD was sorry that He had made man on the earth, and He was grieved in His heart.

7 The LORD said, "I will blot out man whom I have created from the face of the land, from man to animals to creeping things and to birds of the sky; for I am sorry that I have made them."

8 But Noah found favor in the eyes of the LORD.

9 These are the records of the generations of Noah. Noah was a righteous man, blameless in his time; Noah walked with God.

ONE STEP FURTHER:

Noah: The Whole Story

If you have time, read the full account of Noah's life in Genesis 6-9. If you're pressed for time but still want the rest of the story, use an audio Bible! Then record your observations below.

Loving Like
JESUS
In a World that Hurts and Hates

10 *Noah became the father of three sons: Shem, Ham, and Japheth.*

11 *Now the earth was corrupt in the sight of God, and the earth was filled with violence.*

12 *God looked on the earth, and behold, it was corrupt; for all flesh had corrupted their way upon the earth.*

13 *Then God said to Noah, "The end of all flesh has come before Me; for the earth is filled with violence because of them; and behold, I am about to destroy them with the earth.*

14 *"Make for yourself an ark of gopher wood; you shall make the ark with rooms, and shall cover it inside and out with pitch.*

15 *"This is how you shall make it: the length of the ark three hundred cubits, its breadth fifty cubits, and its height thirty cubits.*

16 *"You shall make a window for the ark, and finish it to a cubit from the top; and set the door of the ark in the side of it; you shall make it with lower, second, and third decks.*

17 *"Behold, I, even I am bringing the flood of water upon the earth, to destroy all flesh in which is the breath of life, from under heaven; everything that is on the earth shall perish.*

18 *"But I will establish My covenant with you; and you shall enter the ark—you and your sons and your wife, and your sons' wives with you.*

19 *"And of every living thing of all flesh, you shall bring two of every kind into the ark, to keep them alive with you; they shall be male and female.*

20 *"Of the birds after their kind, and of the animals after their kind, of every creeping thing of the ground after its kind, two of every kind will come to you to keep them alive.*

21 *"As for you, take for yourself some of all food which is edible, and gather it to yourself; and it shall be for food for you and for them."*

22 *Thus Noah did; according to all that God had commanded him, so he did.*

Genesis 7:5-6

5 *Noah did according to all that the LORD had commanded him.*

6 *Now Noah was six hundred years old when the flood of water came upon the earth.*

DISCUSS with your GROUP or PONDER on your own . . .

Make a quick list of all of the time references you noted in the text along with anything you learned from them. Take particular note of time references that imply how long it took Noah to build the ark.

ONE STEP FURTHER:

Beginnings
If you're newer to Bible study, it would be great for you to take the time this week to read the creation account in Genesis 1–3. It will be very helpful in answering some of the Noah comparison questions. Record your observations on the creation account below along with any questions you may need to follow up.

Loving Like
JESUS
In a World that Hurts and Hates

Week Four: **Love Is . . .**

How did the earth at the time of Noah differ from what it was when God created it? How did it change?

How slow to anger did God show Himself to be? What happened?

What was God's purpose in having Noah build an ark?

OBSERVE the TEXT of SCRIPTURE

While Peter's example of God's patience came from the days of Noah, Paul used his own life to show God's patience to "the foremost of all" sinners. Let's take a look.

READ 1 Timothy 1:15-16 and **MARK** every reference to *patience*.

1 Timothy 1:15-16

15 *It is a trustworthy statement, deserving full acceptance, that Christ Jesus came into the world to save sinners, among whom I am foremost of all.*

16 *Yet for this reason I found mercy, so that in me as the foremost, Jesus Christ might demonstrate His perfect patience as an example for those who would believe in Him for eternal life.*

DISCUSS with your GROUP or PONDER on your own . . .

Briefly compare Paul's statement about Christ's work with Peter's (1 Peter 3:18, page 53). Why did Jesus come into the world? For what purpose did He die?

According to Paul, how did Jesus demonstrate His perfect patience? Why did He do it?

How has God demonstrated His perfect patience toward you? Have you ever considered how this should affect the way you treat others? Explain.

OBSERVE the TEXT of SCRIPTURE

Let's take a look at Paul's life prior to Christ to see why he was a perfect object to demonstrate God's perfect patience!

READ Acts 22:1-21 and **UNDERLINE** everything Paul did before he came to know Jesus.

Acts 22:1-21

1 *"Brethren and fathers, hear my defense which I now offer to you."*

2 *And when they heard that he was addressing them in the Hebrew dialect, they became even more quiet; and he said,*

3 *"I am a Jew, born in Tarsus of Cilicia, but brought up in this city, educated under Gamaliel, strictly according to the law of our fathers, being zealous for God just as you all are today.*

4 *"I persecuted this Way to the death, binding and putting both men and women into prisons,*

5 *as also the high priest and all the Council of the elders can testify. From them I also received letters to the brethren, and started off for Damascus in order to bring even those who were there to Jerusalem as prisoners to be punished.*

6 *"But it happened that as I was on my way, approaching Damascus about noontime, a very bright light suddenly flashed from heaven all around me,*

7 *and I fell to the ground and heard a voice saying to me, 'Saul, Saul, why are you persecuting Me?'*

8 *"And I answered, 'Who are You, Lord?' And He said to me, 'I am Jesus the Nazarene, whom you are persecuting.'*

9 *"And those who were with me saw the light, to be sure, but did not understand the voice of the One who was speaking to me.*

10 *"And I said, 'What shall I do, Lord?' And the Lord said to me, 'Get up and go on into Damascus, and there you will be told of all that has been appointed for you to do.'*

ONE STEP FURTHER:

Paul's Story

For more on God's miraculous saving of Paul, check out the following accounts and record what you learn from each.

Acts 9

Acts 26

Galatians 1:13-17

Loving Like JESUS
In a World that Hurts and Hates

11   *"But since I could not see because of the brightness of that light, I was led by the hand by those who were with me and came into Damascus.*

12   *"A certain Ananias, a man who was devout by the standard of the Law, and well spoken of by all the Jews who lived there,*

13   *came to me, and standing near said to me, 'Brother Saul, receive your sight!' And at that very time I looked up at him.*

14   *"And he said, 'The God of our fathers has appointed you to know His will and to see the Righteous One and to hear an utterance from His mouth.*

15   *'For you will be a witness for Him to all men of what you have seen and heard.*

16   *'Now why do you delay? Get up and be baptized, and wash away your sins, calling on His name.'*

17   *"It happened when I returned to Jerusalem and was praying in the temple, that I fell into a trance,*

18   *and I saw Him saying to me, 'Make haste, and get out of Jerusalem quickly, because they will not accept your testimony about Me.'*

19   *"And I said, 'Lord, they themselves understand that in one synagogue after another I used to imprison and beat those who believed in You.*

20   *'And when the blood of Your witness Stephen was being shed, I also was standing by approving, and watching out for the coats of those who were slaying him.'*

21   *"And He said to me, 'Go! For I will send you far away to the Gentiles.' "*

DISCUSS with your GROUP or PONDER on your own . . .

Briefly describe Paul's pre-Jesus life.

How does knowing Paul's backstory help us better understand the perfect patience Jesus showed him?

How can this example encourage those who don't know Jesus? You and me as we live with those who don't yet know Him?

Digging Deeper

Practical Benefits of Patience According to the Proverbs

If you have some extra time on your hands this week, see what the Proverbs have to say about the benefits of patience in a person's life!

Proverbs 14:29

Proverbs 15:18

Proverbs 16:32

Proverbs 17:27

Proverbs 19:8

Proverbs 25:15

Loving Like
JESUS
In a World that Hurts and Hates

KIND

Love is patient, love is kind. We've looked at some examples of God's patience—His "long anger"—with sinners. He is not slow to anger without purpose. He is patient with sinners and His kindness is designed with a specific outcome in mind. Let's look at Romans 2 and Titus 3 to see how God's kindness is tied to His saving purposes.

OBSERVE the TEXT of SCRIPTURE

In Romans 1—3 Paul shows that all people are sinners—those who have never heard about God, those who are "good" or "religious," and even the Jews themselves.

READ Romans 2:1-4 and **MARK** every reference to *kindness* and to *judgment*. Also **MARK** every reference to *God*.

Romans 2:1-4

1 *Therefore you have no excuse, everyone of you who passes judgment, for in that which you judge another, you condemn yourself; for you who judge practice the same things.*

2 *And we know that the judgment of God rightly falls upon those who practice such things.*

3 *But do you suppose this, O man, when you pass judgment on those who practice such things and do the same yourself, that you will escape the judgment of God?*

4 *Or do you think lightly of the riches of His kindness and tolerance and patience, not knowing that the kindness of God leads you to repentance?*

DISCUSS with your GROUP or PONDER on your own . . .

What does the text tell us about God and judgment?

What is God's kindness designed to do? Thinking practically, what would you say to those who think God is "okay" with them because they have a good life?

FYI:

God's Kindness to Evil Men

"But love your enemies, and do good, and lend, expecting nothing in return; and your reward will be great, and you will be sons of the Most High; for He Himself is kind to ungrateful and evil men."

—Jesus, Luke 6:35

If God uses kindness to lead people to repentance—and He does!—how should His children treat people?

Spend some time in prayer asking God to reveal any areas of your life where you need His kindness to permeate your thinking and behavior. Then write down what you need to remember.

> **FYI:**
>
> **Be Kind Like God Is To You**
>
> *Be kind to one another, tender-hearted, forgiving each other, just as God in Christ also has forgiven you.*
>
> —Ephesians 4:32

OBSERVE the TEXT of SCRIPTURE

READ Titus 3:3-7 and **MARK** *kindness*. Then **UNDERLINE** what His kindness did.

Titus 3:3-7

3 *For we also once were foolish ourselves, disobedient, deceived, enslaved to various lusts and pleasures, spending our life in malice and envy, hateful, hating one another.*

4 *But when the kindness of God our Savior and His love for mankind appeared,*

5 *He saved us, not on the basis of deeds which we have done in righteousness, but according to His mercy, by the washing of regeneration and renewing by the Holy Spirit,*

6 *whom He poured out upon us richly through Jesus Christ our Savior,*

7 *so that being justified by His grace we would be made heirs according to the hope of eternal life.*

DISCUSS with your GROUP or PONDER on your own . . .

According to Titus 3:3, what were you like before God saved you?

Loving Like
JESUS
In a World that Hurts and Hates

Week Four: **Love Is . . .**

What did God's kindness do?

Think back to a time in your life when someone acted kindly toward you when you did not deserve it. How did this affect you and your attitude toward that person?

If God's kindness is tied with salvation, can we call ourselves "kind" if we do not share Jesus? Explain.

Think of some ways you can show kindness this week for the sake of Jesus and His Gospel. Write them down and ask God for opportunities!

@THE END OF THE DAY . . .

Love, patience, kindness . . . what a high bar! Paul will continue to paint love's portrait as we move on through this passage and we will continue to see that it is supernatural. You can't do it on your own. The type of love that God desires and commands is the love that He Himself grows in us!

Loving Like
JESUS
In a World that Hurts and Hates

HOW TO PARSE A VERB

For use with www.blueletterbible.org

1. Type in 1 Corinthians 13:4 (or any other verse you're studying). Keep the version as KJV (the function we're using only works with the KJV version at this point.) Click the "Search" button.

2. When you arrive at the next screen, you will see a button labeled "Tools" to the left of your verse.

   Hover over the "Tool" button and a list will pop up.

   Click the first button on the pop-up list—"Interlinear C"—to take you to the concordance link.

3. Scroll down until you see the English and Greek words in parallel columns.

4. In this instance, we are looking for Strong #G3144, *makrothumeo*. Click on the blue "PARSE" button to the right of the word in the Parsing column.

5. The Parsing Information will pop up and show you the Tense, Voice, and Mood of the verb.

Week Five

Love Isn't . . .

*"Love is patient, love is kind and **is not jealous;**
love does not brag and **is not arrogant,**
does not act unbecomingly; it does not seek its own,
is not provoked, does not take into account
a wrong suffered . . . "*
—1 Corinthians 13:4-5

There is a sweetness and kindness to a conversation about what love *is*. Even when we don't quite measure up, there's at least something to aspire to, a better way that calls, the possibility of a brighter tomorrow. When we start discussing what love *isn't*, everything becomes more stark and, at least for me, "measurable." The discussion morphs into something far more tangible because when we talk about what love *is not*, it's easier to see ourselves as offenders. Maybe it's just me, but the truth that "love isn't provoked" hits my core. Hey, misery loves company and so does refining! Join me? It's better on the other side—God isn't going to leave us the way we are!

Loving Like
JESUS
In a World that Hurts and Hates

Week Five: **Love Isn't . . .**

REMEMBERING

Take a few minutes to review what you learned last week about what love *is*.

How has your life been changing as a result of what you've been learning? Give one specific example if you can.

LOVE ISN'T . . .

This week we'll be focusing on what Paul tells us love *isn't*. Remember, we're still dealing with a long string of verbs in the Greek. So while English translations have the adjectives patient, kind, and arrogant, the corresponding Greek terms are verbs: and so "Love 'long-wraths'" (KJV's "long-suffers" is close), favors (does kind things), and does not vaunt (KJV's "puffs up" is literal; brag and boast are close).

. . . JEALOUS

Although the Greek word translated as "jealous" can be used in the positive sense of "zeal," Paul obviously has the negative in mind when he tells his readers that love is not jealous. The term itself is neutral and acquires moral sense in its object.

OBSERVE the TEXT of SCRIPTURE

READ 1 Corinthians 13:4 and **MARK** the phrase *not jealous*.

1 Corinthians 13:4

4 *Love is patient, love is kind* and *is not jealous; love does not brag* and *is not arrogant,*

DISCUSS with your GROUP or PONDER on your own . . .

What words are neighbors of "is not jealous" in 1 Corinthians 13:4? How do you think they interact with one another? (Don't worry, we'll get to the application questions after Genesis 37!)

Loving Like
JESUS
In a World that Hurts and Hates

OBSERVE the TEXT of SCRIPTURE

Stephen refers to the jealousy of Joseph's brothers in his speech in Acts 7. Let's take a look at Joseph's life and how his brothers acted jealously toward him.

READ Genesis 37 and **MARK** every reference to the brothers' feelings toward Joseph.

Genesis 37

1   Now Jacob lived in the land where his father had sojourned, in the land of Canaan.

2   These are the records of *the generations of Jacob.*

Joseph, when seventeen years of age, was pasturing the flock with his brothers while he was still a youth, along with the sons of Bilhah and the sons of Zilpah, his father's wives. And Joseph brought back a bad report about them to their father.

3   Now Israel loved Joseph more than all his sons, because he was the son of his old age; and he made him a varicolored tunic.

4   His brothers saw that their father loved him more than all his brothers; and so they hated him and could not speak to him on friendly terms.

5   Then Joseph had a dream, and when he told it to his brothers, they hated him even more.

6   He said to them, "Please listen to this dream which I have had;

7   for behold, we were binding sheaves in the field, and lo, my sheaf rose up and also stood erect; and behold, your sheaves gathered around and bowed down to my sheaf."

8   Then his brothers said to him, "Are you actually going to reign over us? Or are you really going to rule over us?" So they hated him even more for his dreams and for his words.

9   Now he had still another dream, and related it to his brothers, and said, "Lo, I have had still another dream; and behold, the sun and the moon and eleven stars were bowing down to me."

10 He related it to his father and to his brothers; and his father rebuked him and said to him, "What is this dream that you have had? Shall I and your mother and your brothers actually come to bow ourselves down before you to the ground?"

11 His brothers were jealous of him, but his father kept the saying in mind.

12 Then his brothers went to pasture their father's flock in Shechem.

13 Israel said to Joseph, "Are not your brothers pasturing the flock in Shechem? Come, and I will send you to them." And he said to him, "I will go."

14 Then he said to him, "Go now and see about the welfare of your brothers and the welfare of the flock, and bring word back to me." So he sent him from the valley of Hebron, and he came to Shechem.

15 A man found him, and behold, he was wandering in the field; and the man asked him, "What are you looking for?"

ONE STEP FURTHER:

Word Study: Jealous, NT

If you have some extra time this week, see if you can discover the Greek words for "jealous" and "jealousy." When you do, write them down along with any information you discover about how they're used in the Corinthian letters, elsewhere in Paul's writings, and elsewhere in the New Testament. While you're at it, you may want to see how and where the words are used in the *LXX*, the Greek translation of the Old Testament.

Loving Like JESUS
In a World that Hurts and Hates

Week Five: **Love Isn't . . .**

ONE STEP FURTHER:

Word Study: Jealous, OT

If you enjoyed searching for information about jealousy in the New Testament, take some time to discover what you can about jealousy in the Old Testament. The main Hebrew words are *qana* (H7065, a verb, "to be jealous"), *qanna* (H7067, an adjective, "jealous"), and *qinah* (H7068, a noun, "jealousy"). See what you can find out about where they are used, who they refer to, and anything else of interest. Then record your findings below as well as any questions that may come up!

16 He said, "I am looking for my brothers; please tell me where they are pasturing the flock."

17 Then the man said, "They have moved from here; for I heard them say, 'Let us go to Dothan.' " So Joseph went after his brothers and found them at Dothan.

18 When they saw him from a distance and before he came close to them, they plotted against him to put him to death.

19 They said to one another, "Here comes this dreamer!

20 "Now then, come and let us kill him and throw him into one of the pits; and we will say, 'A wild beast devoured him.' Then let us see what will become of his dreams!"

21 But Reuben heard this and rescued him out of their hands and said, "Let us not take his life."

22 Reuben further said to them, "Shed no blood. Throw him into this pit that is in the wilderness, but do not lay hands on him"—that he might rescue him out of their hands, to restore him to his father.

23 So it came about, when Joseph reached his brothers, that they stripped Joseph of his tunic, the varicolored tunic that was on him;

24 and they took him and threw him into the pit. Now the pit was empty, without any water in it.

25 Then they sat down to eat a meal. And as they raised their eyes and looked, behold, a caravan of Ishmaelites was coming from Gilead, with their camels bearing aromatic gum and balm and myrrh, on their way to bring them down to Egypt.

26 Judah said to his brothers, "What profit is it for us to kill our brother and cover up his blood?

27 "Come and let us sell him to the Ishmaelites and not lay our hands on him, for he is our brother, our own flesh." And his brothers listened to him.

28 Then some Midianite traders passed by, so they pulled him up and lifted Joseph out of the pit, and sold him to the Ishmaelites for twenty shekels of silver. Thus they brought Joseph into Egypt.

29 Now Reuben returned to the pit, and behold, Joseph was not in the pit; so he tore his garments.

30 He returned to his brothers and said, "The boy is not there; as for me, where am I to go?"

31 So they took Joseph's tunic, and slaughtered a male goat and dipped the tunic in the blood;

32 and they sent the varicolored tunic and brought it to their father and said, "We found this; please examine it to see whether it is your son's tunic or not."

33 Then he examined it and said, "It is my son's tunic. A wild beast has devoured him; Joseph has surely been torn to pieces!"

34 So Jacob tore his clothes, and put sackcloth on his loins and mourned for his son many days.

35 *Then all his sons and all his daughters arose to comfort him, but he refused to be comforted. And he said, "Surely I will go down to Sheol in mourning for my son." So his father wept for him.*

36 *Meanwhile, the Midianites sold him in Egypt to Potiphar, Pharaoh's officer, the captain of the bodyguard.*

FYI:

A Name Change
God changed Jacob's name to Israel (see Genesis 35:10). "Israel" in Genesis 37:3 is the "Jacob" used elsewhere in the chapter.

DISCUSS with your GROUP or PONDER on your own . . .

Let's briefly review the account . . .

Describe Joseph using your markings in the text as a guide. You may want to make a list.

What was Israel's (aka Jacob's) relationship with his son Joseph like? Why was it like this?

What did Joseph's brothers think about him? How did this affect their relationship?

How does Genesis 37:11 describe the brothers' disposition toward Joseph?

How did jealousy drive the brothers' actions? What did they end up doing? What did they *want* to do?

Loving Like
JESUS
In a World that Hurts and Hates

Week Five: **Love Isn't . . .**

How did the brothers' jealousy hurt Joseph? How did it hurt Joseph's father?

If you know the rest of the story, how did their jealousy hurt them, too?

Think for a moment about your life. How has your jealously of others hurt you? What about others you know? (Remember, when we confess, God is faithful and righteous to forgive us and cleanse us from all unrighteousness [1 John 1:9], so don't let this be a time of self-flagellation but of reflecting so you can walk forward better.)

Have you ever been hurt by the jealousy of others? If so, how? What can you learn from this that you can apply to your behavior with others?

ONE STEP FURTHER:

Jealousy in Acts

If you have a little extra time, check out Acts 17:1-9 where a group becomes jealous of the ministry of Paul and Silas. As you read, watch to see WHO is jealous, WHAT they are jealous about, WHEN they become jealous, WHERE all this happens, HOW they act, and WHY they behave like they do. Record below what you learn from actively reading and questioning the text.

OBSERVE the TEXT of SCRIPTURE

James has some get-in-your-business talk about where jealousy comes from . . . and it's not pretty. While this section of text is packed with wisdom, we're going to focus our attention on what James says specifically about jealousy!

READ James 3:13–4:3 and **MARK** the words *jealousy* and *envious*.

James 3:13–4:3

13 *Who among you is wise and understanding? Let him show by his good behavior his deeds in the gentleness of wisdom.*

14 *But if you have bitter jealousy and selfish ambition in your heart, do not be arrogant and so lie against the truth.*

15 This wisdom is not that which comes down from above, but is earthly, natural, demonic.

16 For where jealousy and selfish ambition exist, there is disorder and every evil thing.

17 But the wisdom from above is first pure, then peaceable, gentle, reasonable, full of mercy and good fruits, unwavering, without hypocrisy.

18 And the seed whose fruit is righteousness is sown in peace by those who make peace.

4:1 What is the source of quarrels and conflicts among you? Is not the source your pleasures that wage war in your members?

2 You lust and do not have; so you commit murder. You are envious and cannot obtain; so you fight and quarrel. You do not have because you do not ask.

3 You ask and do not receive, because you ask with wrong motives, so that you may spend it on your pleasures.

DISCUSS with your GROUP or PONDER on your own . . .

What is jealousy's "best friend" in the text? How do they go together?

What do these have to do with arrogant behavior?

Where do jealousy and selfish ambition come from? What company do they keep?

According to James 4:2, what results when we envy or covet (as the *ESV* here translates the Greek *zeloo*)?

Loving Like
JESUS
In a World that Hurts and Hates

Week Five: **Love Isn't . . .**

Think for a moment to the last time you were in a tiff with someone. Did jealousy have anything to do with it? If so, how?

What are practical ways you can identify jealousy in your life? According to the text, what are some indicators you can look for?

What are some specific ways God has helped you overcome and have victory over jealous behavior?

. . . ARROGANT

OBSERVE the TEXT of SCRIPTURE

READ 1 Corinthians 13:4 and **MARK** the phrase *is not arrogant.*

1 Corinthians 13:4

4 *Love is patient, love is kind* and *is not jealous; love does not brag* and *is not arrogant,*

DISCUSS with your GROUP or PONDER on your own . . .

How does the truth "love . . . is not arrogant" fit the other descriptions of love in this verse? Does it correlate with any one more than the others? Explain.

OBSERVE the TEXT of SCRIPTURE

If ever there were a "Corinthian" word, *arrogant* would be it! In fact, arrogant (from the Greek verb *phusioo*) appears only seven times in the New Testament and *six* of them are in 1 Corinthians! Let's take a look at each of these 1 Corinthian uses to see what Paul says about arrogance and about how people become arrogant.

READ 1 Corinthians 4:6-7 and **MARK** the word *arrogant*. **UNDERLINE** any words that Paul associates with it.

1 Corinthians 4:6-7

6 *Now these things, brethren, I have figuratively applied to myself and Apollos for your sakes, so that in us you may learn not to exceed what is written, so that no one of you will become arrogant in behalf of one against the other.*

7 *For who regards you as superior? What do you have that you did not receive? And if you did receive it, why do you boast as if you had not received it?*

DISCUSS with your GROUP or PONDER on your own . . .

What should the Corinthians not do? What do you think Paul is referring to?

What can this lead to? Why?

What does Paul ask in verse 7? What answers is he expecting? How do you think this ties in with his instruction in verse 6?

Can you think of any examples of this today?

FYI:

Arrogant in Colossians

The word translated "arrogant" in 1 Corinthians (the Greek verb *phusioo*, I blow) is translated "inflated" in Colossians 2:18-19. Let's take a look:

"Let no one keep defrauding you of your prize by delighting in self-abasement and the worship of the angels, taking his stand on visions he has seen, inflated without cause by his fleshly mind, and not holding fast to the head, from whom the entire body, being supplied and held together by the joints and ligaments, grows with a growth which is from God."

This usage is similar to Paul's description of arrogance in 1 Corinthians 4:6 where he talks about going beyond what is written. Some of the Colossians puffed themselves up because they claimed to receive revelation in visions that was more than the faith once for all delivered to the saints (Jude 3).

Loving Like
JESUS
In a World that Hurts and Hates

Week Five: **Love Isn't . . .**

Do you ever "exceed what is written" or exalt those who do? Explain.

OBSERVE the TEXT of SCRIPTURE

READ 1 Corinthians 4:18-21 and again **MARK** the word *arrogant.* **UNDERLINE** any words that Paul associates with it.

1 Corinthians 4:18-21

18 *Now some have become arrogant, as though I were not coming to you.*

19 *But I will come to you soon, if the Lord wills, and I shall find out, not the words of those who are arrogant but their power.*

20 *For the kingdom of God does not consist in words but in power.*

21 *What do you desire? Shall I come to you with a rod, or with love and a spirit of gentleness?*

DISCUSS with your GROUP or PONDER on your own . . .

What does the Corinthians' arrogance reveal about them and their relationship to Paul? What purpose do you think stands behind this?

What does the kingdom of God consist of?

What do arrogance and words have to do with one another? Have you ever noticed arrogance and words tied together in your life? If so, how?

OBSERVE the TEXT of SCRIPTURE

READ 1 Corinthians 5:1-2 and **MARK** the word *arrogant.* **UNDERLINE** any words that Paul associates with it.

1 Corinthians 5:1-2

1   It is actually reported that there is immorality among you, and immorality of such a kind as does not exist even among the Gentiles, that someone has his father's wife.

2   You have become arrogant and have not mourned instead, so that the one who had done this deed would be removed from your midst.

DISCUSS with your GROUP or PONDER on your own . . .

What does Paul call the Corinthians out on?

What should their response to this sin have been? Instead, what did they do? What term does Paul use to describe what they have become?

What sins do we, our churches, and society no longer mourn?

If love is not arrogant and arrogance ignores sin, what does this imply about biblical love's proper response toward sin? (Remember the context here. Paul is talking about what should happen among professing believers, not society at large.)

FYI:

Blessed Are Those . . .

"Blessed are those who mourn, for they shall be comforted."

—Jesus, Matthew 5:4

Jesus refers to a mourning over sin related to being poor in spirit (v. 3).

Loving Like
JESUS
In a World that Hurts and Hates

75

Week Five: **Love Isn't . . .**

OBSERVE the TEXT of SCRIPTURE

Paul's comments on knowledge and love in this section appear within a very specific argument regarding whether or not people could, with a clear conscience, eat foods that had previously been sacrificed to idols. Thus, as we answer the questions that follow, we need to realize that "knowledge" in this text has to do with people who are behaving in a way that is doctrinally sound—they have the correct perspective on food offered to idols—but they are missing the mark because they don't care how their informed behavior affects others. Whatever you do, don't read Paul saying that knowing truth is not important. Remember, Jesus told the Jews who believed in Him that they would know the truth and that the truth would make them free (John 8:32)!

READ 1 Corinthians 8:1-3 and **MARK** the word *arrogant*. Also **MARK** every reference to *knowledge* (also *know, knows, known*).

1 Corinthians 8:1-3

1   *Now concerning things sacrificed to idols, we know that we all have knowledge. Knowledge makes arrogant, but love edifies.*

2   *If anyone supposes that he knows anything, he has not yet known as he ought to know;*

3   *but if anyone loves God, he is known by Him.*

DISCUSS with your GROUP or PONDER on your own . . .

Make a short list of everything you learned by marking "knowledge" words in the text.

What does Paul say about people who think they know things?

If knowledge is divorced from love, what will it do? By contrast, what does love do?

How have you seen knowledge and love working together and working apart? You may want to consider Ephesians 4:15 as you answer.

Finally, think through everything you've seen in 1 Corinthians about arrogance. How would you define arrogance based on the texts?

Do any of the components of arrogance that Paul mentioned apply to you? If so, what? What adjustments do you need to bring your thinking in line with God's Word and ways?

Digging Deeper

Knowing Truth for Yourself

If you have some extra time this week, do some research to see what God's Word has to say about the importance of knowing God through His Word. Use a concordance to get started by searching on *know* (put it in like this—know*—and it will search other forms of the word, too) and *truth* (also search *true*). But don't be limited by them. Go to it and think for yourself! Then record below what you learn.

FYI:

The Truth Will Set You Free

So Jesus was saying to those Jews who had believed Him, "If you continue in My word, then you are truly disciples of Mine; and you will know the truth, and the truth will make you free."

—John 8:31-32

Loving Like
JESUS
In a World that Hurts and Hates

ONE STEP FURTHER:

Acts 17:16-34

If you have some extra time, check out how Paul was provoked (in a positive way) in Acts 17:16-34 and note what he did about it. Record your findings below.

Week Five: **Love Isn't . . .**

. . . PROVOKED

Do you ever feel like you'd be just fine in life if people didn't keep pushing your buttons all day, everyday? I'm not proud of this, but I can't tell you how many times I've thought to myself, "I'd live a much better 'Christian' life if only I didn't have to deal with . . . ." Long story short: love deactivates the buttons! The button that used to set me off won't yield the same results when I'm walking in love.

OBSERVE the TEXT of SCRIPTURE

READ 1 Corinthians 13:5 and **MARK** the phrase *is not provoked.*

1 Corinthians 13:5

> 5 *does not act unbecomingly; it does not seek its own, is not provoked, does not take into account a wrong* suffered,

DISCUSS with your GROUP or PONDER on your own . . .

What neighbors does "love . . . is not provoked" keep? Do any of them seem related? If so, how?

Do you ever find yourself getting worked up because something or someone "happened" to you? What is your typical internal conversation when someone is the catalyst for you becoming agitated or angry? Do you take responsibility or shift it to the agitator? Why?

Does 1 Corinthians address the agitator? Who does it address? How many parties are there to a provocation? What happens if the "provoked" chooses not to react?

Can you think of any other characteristics of love that would help a person not be provoked? Explain.

What is the verb tense of "is not provoked"? What does it imply? (Use BlueLetterBible.org to answer. Refer back to page 63 for help.)

OBSERVE the TEXT of SCRIPTURE

Like other neutral words, biblical and otherwise, "provoke" can have negative and positive attachments to anger or to something good. Paul uses a negative connotation in 1 Corinthians 13:5. The author of Hebrews uses it in a positive sense when he says in Hebrews 10:24 that believers should "consider how to stimulate [Greek: *paroxusmos*] one another to love and good deeds."

Let's look at Acts 15 to see how Paul and Barnabas dealt with a provocation (Greek: *paroxusmos*, translated here as "sharp disagreement") between them.

READ Acts 15:36-41 and **MARK** distinctly references to *Paul* and *Barnabas*.

Acts 15:36-41

36 *After some days Paul said to Barnabas, "Let us return and visit the brethren in every city in which we proclaimed the word of the Lord, and see how they are."*

37 *Barnabas wanted to take John, called Mark, along with them also.*

38 *But Paul kept insisting that they should not take him along who had deserted them in Pamphylia and had not gone with them to the work.*

39 *And there occurred such a sharp disagreement that they separated from one another, and Barnabas took Mark with him and sailed away to Cyprus.*

40 *But Paul chose Silas and left, being committed by the brethren to the grace of the Lord.*

41 *And he was traveling through Syria and Cilicia, strengthening the churches.*

Loving Like
JESUS
In a World that Hurts and Hates

Week Five: **Love Isn't . . .**

DISCUSS with your GROUP or PONDER on your own . . .

What did Paul and Barnabas disagree about?

How did Paul support his view?

What did Barnabas want to do?

In the phase "there occurred such a sharp disagreement," what is the tense of the verb and what difference does it make? (Again, use BlueLetterBible.org.)

How does the verb tense here differ from that of "love is not provoked" in 1 Corinthians 13?

What are some practical ways you can keep yourself from being provoked?

What are some ways you can keep yourself from remaining provoked?

@THE END OF THE DAY . . .

Before you call it a day, spend some time talking to God and then write down anything you need to remember about ridding jealousy, arrogance, and provocation from your life. You are not alone. He will help root it out.

Week Five: **Love Isn't . . .**

Week Six

Love Doesn't . . .

> "*. . . love* **does not brag** *and is not arrogant,*
> **does not act unbecomingly;** *it* **does not seek its own,** *is not*
> *provoked,* **does not take into account a wrong** *suffered,*
> **does not rejoice in unrighteousness** *. . ."*
> —1 Corinthians 13:4b-6a

Before we get back to the positive side and look at what love does, we're going to finish up looking at the "negatives." Last week we considered what love "isn't"; this week we're going to unpack what love "doesn't." The negatives help us see love in three dimensions. Artists often talk about positive and negative spaces. The negative, what isn't there, is just as important in defining art, and reality for that matter, as what is. So let's look at each of these phrases carefully and take them to heart because what love doesn't do is every bit as defining and compelling as what it does do . . . and again, none of this is rooted in moralism or just-try-harder grit. Rather, it is a result of the Spirit living in believers and believers living in submission to Him! More on that later, but we can't remind ourselves of this truth often enough!

Loving Like
JESUS
In a World that Hurts and Hates

Week Six: **Love Doesn't . . .**

REMEMBERING

Briefly summarize what you've learned so far.

What has been the most significant change in your thinking or behavior?

See if you can remember the gifts Paul talked about in 1 Corinthians 13:1-3 and the results of those gifts apart from love.

Gift	+ No Love	= Result

FYI:

Getting it "Wrong"

Sometimes we're tempted to correct our memory work as we go, checking word by word for errors. I'd like to suggest that you write it all out the best you can—like you're taking an exam—and see how you do. What I've found over the years, is that I tend to have greater recall of things I've gotten wrong in the past. When you write out verses, it is very easy to see what you're missing and it's easy to identify repeating mistakes. Ask me what the Greek word *logizomai* means. I'll take that definition to my grave because it was an answer that I got wrong on a test as a sophomore in college!

Now, recap 1 Corinthians 13:1-3. If you've memorized it, write it down word for word. If you've decided to memorize general content, write that down. (If you've memorized and aren't sure if you've got it, use a pencil and go back and correct it instead of checking as you go. You'll tend to remember things you've gotten "wrong"—at least I do!)

Write down what "Love is . . ."

Write down what "Love isn't"

If you've already memorized 1 Corinthians 13:4-7, write it from memory below. If you haven't, go ahead and write it out by looking at the text. I'd suggest writing it as many times as you can fit on this page. As you do, pay attention to patterns that can help you memorize.

FYI:

Write It, Say It, Practice It
There's no "right" way to memorize. It just takes time. In fact, often when we think we'll never get it, we're actually very close! Just keep plugging along by reading aloud, writing, reciting, etc. etc. etc. and you'll get it eventually . . . maybe not all of it and maybe not word for word, but you'll still be hiding God's living and active Word in your heart!

Loving Like
JESUS
In a World that Hurts and Hates

Digging Deeper

Memorizing

Patterns are important in the early stages of memorizing. You probably won't remember them after the fact, but then you won't need to. Before you have a passage "down cold," though, patterns help you think through what is next in the text. Here are some of the patterns and "memory hooks" that I've used for 1 Corinthians 13:1-3.

1 Corinthians 13:1-3

Key ideas. #Nothing #Love #SpiritualGifts

1. (Memory Hooks: one gift; "I speak but become noisy")

If I _____ (gift), but do not have love, I _____(result).

2. (Memory Hooks: three gifts; "all" used three times; "I KNOW all, but AM nothing")

If I _____ (gift)

and _____ and _____ (gift),

and

if I _____(gift), but do not have love, I _____ (result).

3. (Memory Hooks: one gift, two examples; "all" used once; "I GIVE all but do not profit AT all")

And

if I _____ (gift)

and

if I _____ (gift), but do not have love, it _____ (result).

Look for patterns on your own in 1 Corinthians 13:4-7 and write them below. You'll remember them better if you find them on your own. I'll share mine with you next week in case you're having trouble.

LOVE DOESN'T . . .

All of love's characteristics that we've been studying fall into the category of Greek verbs even though they're disguised as other parts of speech in English. As you'll recall, we've already seen that love isn't jealous, arrogant, or provoked! Today we'll add that it doesn't brag, act unbecomingly, seek its own, account wrongs, or rejoice in unrighteousness. Let's get going, we have miles to cover!

. . . BRAG

Because the word translated "brag" (Greek: *perpereuomai*) appears only once in the New Testament, we can't cross-reference to see how it's used elsewhere. Likely, though, *ou perpereuomai* shows an opposite characteristic, a corrective to the Corinthians' arrogant speech.

Let's compare 1 Corinthians 13:4 with two verses earlier in the letter that point to this exalted speech. Apparently this group talked a big game!

OBSERVE the TEXT of SCRIPTURE

READ the texts and **MARK** every phrase that refers to puffed-up speech.

1 Corinthians 13:4

4 *Love is patient, love is kind* and *is not jealous; love does not brag* and *is not arrogant,*

1 Corinthians 1:17

17 *For Christ did not send me to baptize, but to preach the gospel, not in cleverness of speech, so that the cross of Christ would not be made void.*

1 Corinthians 2:1

1 *And when I came to you, brethren, I did not come with superiority of speech or of wisdom, proclaiming to you the testimony of God.*

DISCUSS with your GROUP or PONDER on your own . . .

List the phrases that you marked.

FYI:

Hapax Legomenon

The Greek phrase "hapax legomenon" is used to describe words that appear only once in the Bible. *Perpereuomai*, translated "brag" in 1 Corinthians 13:4 falls into this category. Typically when we study God's Word, we can compare how words are used in different places to drill down more accurately to the original meaning. When words occur only once in the Bible, translators have to look more closely at how the word was used in secular writings and they also have to pay closer attention to the company the word is keeping in its context. Love does not "brag," for instance, sits next door to the truth that "love is not arrogant." Given the usage of *perpereuomai* in secular Greek and the textual neighbor "love is not arrogant," the translation that "love does not brag," is well supported.

Loving Like
JESUS
In a World that Hurts and Hates

Week Six: **Love Doesn't . . .**

How does Paul describe his speech in 1 Corinthians 1:17 and 2:1? What did he talk about? What does he contrast it with?

FYI:

Text Comparison

While looking at the original languages is typically the best way to help us understand what a word means, checking out other English translations can be helpful, too. Here are how several of the top translations treat the Greek phrase *ou perpereuomai:*

NASB	doesn't brag
ESV	doesn't boast
NIV	doesn't boast
NKJV	doesn't parade itself
NLT	is not . . . boastful

What is his concern with "cleverness of speech"?

Where does Paul's power in his speech come from? (See Romans 1:16-17.)

ONE STEP FURTHER:

Just for Fun . . .
Who does the Bible say "was" the most humble man on the face of the earth?

Do you ever shrink back from sharing the Gospel because you feel your speech isn't up to snuff? What can you learn from Paul's example in this?

Conversely, if you think you're "all that" and are constantly using your mouth to tell people, what message is there for you about how love behaves? What does this have to do with arrogance?

. . . ACT UNBECOMINGLY

"Unbecoming" to an English speaker usually conjures up ideas of clothing that doesn't fit or flatter. For example, "That dress was unbecoming on her." Paul's usage strikes far deeper. In addition to 1 Corinthians 13:5, Paul uses the word we translate "unbecoming" (Greek: *aschmoneo* [verb] and *aschemosune* [noun]) to address inappropriateness that involves a sexual element—one has to do with heterosexual behavior, the other with homosexual actions. Let's compare for ourselves how these other usages help us understand 1 Corinthians 13:5.

OBSERVE the TEXT of SCRIPTURE

READ 1 Corinthians 13:5 and 1 Corinthians 7:36-38. Then **MARK** the phrases *act unbecomingly* and *not behaving properly* which translate the same Greek word: *aschmoneo.*

1 Corinthians 13:5

5 *does not act unbecomingly; it does not seek its own, is not provoked, does not take into account a wrong* suffered,

1 Corinthians 7:36-38

36 *But if any man thinks that he is acting unbecomingly toward his virgin daughter, if she is past her youth, and if it must be so, let him do what he wishes, he does not sin; let her marry.*

37 *But he who stands firm in his heart, being under no constraint, but has authority over his own will, and has decided this in his own heart, to keep his own virgin daughter, he will do well.*

38 *So then both he who gives his own virgin daughter in marriage does well, and he who does not give her in marriage will do better.*

1 Corinthians 7:36-38, ESV

36 *If anyone thinks that he is not behaving properly toward his betrothed, if his passions are strong, and it has to be, let him do as he wishes: let them marry—it is no sin.*

37 *But whoever is firmly established in his heart, being under no necessity but having his desire under control, and has determined this in his heart, to keep her as his betrothed, he will do well.*

38 *So then he who marries his betrothed does well, and he who refrains from marriage will do even better.*

DISCUSS with your GROUP or PONDER on your own . . .

In what context is "not behaving properly" used in 1 Corinthians 7:36?

What is Paul's suggestion to remedy this situation of "not behaving properly"?

FYI:

Why the ESV?
I've added the English Standard Version for 1 Corinthians 7:36-38 so you can see the two divergent ways this text is translated. The NASB translates the word *parthenos* (virgin or maiden) as "virgin *daughter.*" The ESV translates the same word as "betrothed." Literally the Greek reads only "his virgin."

The NASB translators think the comment is directed at a father who is acting unbecomingly by not allowing his daughter to marry and thus bringing on her the reproach of childlessness.

ESV translators think the comment is directed at a young man engaged to be married to "his virgin."

Given the larger context that includes 1 Corinthians 7:9 where Paul counsels "It is better to marry than to burn [with passion]," I lean toward the ESV.

Loving Like
JESUS
In a World that Hurts and Hates

Week Six: **Love Doesn't . . .**

Given what Paul says in 1 Corinthians 13:5, how will *agape* love behave when faced with sexual temptation? What are some ways this is applicable today?

ONE STEP FURTHER:

Romans 1: Get the Context

If you have time this week, read all of Romans 1 so you'll better understand the context of the "unbecoming" behavior, the indecent acts Paul refers to in Romans 1:27. Then record your observations below.

OBSERVE the TEXT of SCRIPTURE

Let's see what "unbecoming" is associated with in another text. In Romans Paul gives an example of "unbecoming" behavior. Having explained that the wrath of God is being revealed against men who reject clearly revealed truth (Romans 1:18ff), Paul cites "indecent acts" (Greek noun: *aschemosune*) in Romans 1:27 as an example of how some truth rejecters live. We need to be clear here that Romans 1:26-27 is *one example* of "unbecoming" behavior—there are plenty of other ways to act unbecomingly—but it is a particularly relevant one to the days in which we live. Let's take a look.

READ Romans 1:22-27 and **MARK** the phrase *indecent acts* (Greek: *aschemosune*). Also, **UNDERLINE** everything these people do.

Romans 1:22-27

22 *Professing to be wise, they became fools,*

23 *and exchanged the glory of the incorruptible God for an image in the form of corruptible man and of birds and four-footed animals and crawling creatures.*

24 *Therefore God gave them over in the lusts of their hearts to impurity, so that their bodies would be dishonored among them.*

25 *For they exchanged the truth of God for a lie, and worshiped and served the creature rather than the Creator, who is blessed forever. Amen.*

26 *For this reason God gave them over to degrading passions; for their women exchanged the natural function for that which is unnatural,*

27 *and in the same way also the men abandoned the natural function of the woman and burned in their desire toward one another, men with men committing indecent acts and receiving in their own persons the due penalty of their error.*

DISCUSS with your GROUP or PONDER on your own . . .

How are the people in Romans 1:22-27 described? What are they like? What do they do?

What things do they trade? What do they exchange them for?

What repeated phrase describes God's response to the people's actions? How many times does it show up?

What does God give these people over to? What does *this* lead to?

What is Paul referring to by "unbecoming" or "indecent acts" in verses 26 and 27? Explain your reasoning from the text.

Using God's 1 Corinthians 13:5 definition of love, can Romans 1:26-27 behavior fit under love's umbrella or is it something else? Again, explain your view from Scripture. As you do, remember the entire topic of this study!!

By contrast, how does God define this behavior and the feelings leading to it in verses 26 and 27?

ONE STEP FURTHER:

Word Studies

If you have extra time this week, investigate some of the words associated with God giving people over. Here are a few phrases you might want to look into:

lusts of their hearts

impurity

dishonored

degrading passions

burned

desire

depraved mind

When you finish, compare what you've seen with Paul's definition of love in 1 Corinthians 13. Then record your observations below.

Loving Like
JESUS
In a World that Hurts and Hates

Week Six: **Love Doesn't . . .**

How can you use God's truth from Romans 1 and 1 Corinthians 13 in our culture . . . and how can you do it in a way that is patient, kind, not provoked, etc.? Take some time on this. Pray and think through some different scenarios. Then jot down your thoughts.

ONE STEP FURTHER:

Elsewhere in Corinthians!
If you have some extra time this week, see what Paul says believers should seek and consider how you can apply what he says.

1 Corinthians 10:23-24

1 Corinthians 14:12

. . . SEEK ITS OWN

Oh my, now we're hitting close to home. Culture's siren song of "Look out for number one!" preaches culture's gospel that "If you don't look out for you, no one will." Paul says love doesn't seek its own. Jesus shows the picture of perfect love that seeks and saves the lost and He warns His followers of the grim reality in seeking wrong things. Let's take a look.

OBSERVE the TEXT of SCRIPTURE

Note that in the Luke 17 passage, Jesus is talking to His disciples about His return.

READ 1 Corinthians 13:5 and Luke 17:26-35 and **MARK** *seeks*.

READ Matthew 14:24-26 and **MARK** *wishes*. This is a different Greek word (*thelo*) but it carries the same idea in this context as *seeks* (*zeteo*) does in the other passages.

1 Corinthians 13:5

5   *does not act unbecomingly; it does not seek its own, is not provoked, does not take into account a wrong suffered,*

Luke 17:26-35

26   *"And just as it happened in the days of Noah, so it will be also in the days of the Son of Man:*

27   *they were eating, they were drinking, they were marrying, they were being given in marriage, until the day that Noah entered the ark, and the flood came and destroyed them all.*

28   *"It was the same as happened in the days of Lot: they were eating, they were drinking, they were buying, they were selling, they were planting, they were building;*

29   *but on the day that Lot went out from Sodom it rained fire and brimstone from heaven and destroyed them all.*

30   *"It will be just the same on the day that the Son of Man is revealed.*

31 *"On that day, the one who is on the housetop and whose goods are in the house must not go down to take them out; and likewise the one who is in the field must not turn back.*

32 *"Remember Lot's wife.*

33 *"Whoever seeks to keep his life will lose it, and whoever loses his life will preserve it.*

34 *"I tell you, on that night there will be two in one bed; one will be taken and the other will be left.*

35 *"There will be two women grinding at the same place; one will be taken and the other will be left.*

Matthew 16:24-26

24 *Then Jesus said to His disciples, "If anyone wishes to come after Me, he must deny himself, and take up his cross and follow Me.*

25 *"For whoever wishes to save his life will lose it; but whoever loses his life for My sake will find it.*

26 *"For what will it profit a man if he gains the whole world and forfeits his soul? Or what will a man give in exchange for his soul?*

DISCUSS with your GROUP or PONDER on your own . . .

How does culture tell us to "seek our own," to "look out for number one"? Do you find it hard to fight against this message? Why?

Compare the contexts of these Luke 17 and Matthew 16 passages. What is similar? What is different?

According to both passages, what counter-intuitive move will cause you to lose your life? How can you save it?

ONE STEP FURTHER:

What the Son Sought

"For the Son of Man has come to seek and to save that which was lost."

—Jesus, Luke 19:10

If you have a few minutes, look up John 5:30 to see what else Jesus sought. Record below what you find and how you will apply it.

Loving Like
JESUS
In a World that Hurts and Hates

Week Six: **Love Doesn't . . .**

What does Jesus tell His disciples is involved in following Him? How does this fit with 1 Corinthians 13?

What difference has following Jesus made in your life?

. . . TAKE INTO ACCOUNT A WRONG SUFFERED

Last week we learned that love isn't provoked. This week Paul tells us that "love does not take into account a wrong suffered." Don't know about you, but even when I don't outwardly retaliate to a provocation, left to my own devices I tend to turn into a tax-season accountant tallying wrongs with both speed and accuracy! But that is not God's way for us. In fact, God Himself demonstrated this for us when instead of accounting our sin against us, He credited (Greek: *logizomai*) those who believe with Christ's righteousness. Let's go to one of the greatest chapters in the Bible . . . Romans 4!

OBSERVE the TEXT of SCRIPTURE

READ 1 Corinthians 13:5 and Romans 4. Then **MARK** every reference to *take into account* and *credited*.

1 Corinthians 13:5

5 *does not act unbecomingly; it does not seek its own, is not provoked, does not take into account a wrong* suffered,

Romans 4

1 *What then shall we say that Abraham, our forefather according to the flesh, has found?*

2 *For if Abraham was justified by works, he has something to boast about, but not before God.*

3 *For what does the Scripture say? "ABRAHAM BELIEVED GOD, AND IT WAS CREDITED TO HIM AS RIGHTEOUSNESS."*

4 *Now to the one who works, his wage is not credited as a favor, but as what is due.*

5   *But to the one who does not work, but believes in Him who justifies the ungodly, his faith is credited as righteousness,*

6   *just as David also speaks of the blessing on the man to whom God credits righteousness apart from works:*

7   *"BLESSED ARE THOSE WHOSE LAWLESS DEEDS HAVE BEEN FORGIVEN,*

    AND WHOSE SINS HAVE BEEN COVERED.

8   *"BLESSED IS THE MAN WHOSE SIN THE LORD WILL NOT TAKE INTO ACCOUNT."*

9   *Is this blessing then on the circumcised, or on the uncircumcised also? For we say, "FAITH WAS CREDITED TO ABRAHAM AS RIGHTEOUSNESS."*

10 *How then was it credited? While he was circumcised, or uncircumcised? Not while circumcised, but while uncircumcised;*

11 *and he received the sign of circumcision, a seal of the righteousness of the faith which he had while uncircumcised, so that he might be the father of all who believe without being circumcised, that righteousness might be credited to them,*

12 *and the father of circumcision to those who not only are of the circumcision, but who also follow in the steps of the faith of our father Abraham which he had while uncircumcised.*

13 *For the promise to Abraham or to his descendants that he would be heir of the world was not through the Law, but through the righteousness of faith.*

14 *For if those who are of the Law are heirs, faith is made void and the promise is nullified;*

15 *for the Law brings about wrath, but where there is no law, there also is no violation.*

16 *For this reason it is by faith, in order that it may be in accordance with grace, so that the promise will be guaranteed to all the descendants, not only to those who are of the Law, but also to those who are of the faith of Abraham, who is the father of us all,*

17 *(as it is written, "A FATHER OF MANY NATIONS HAVE I MADE YOU") in the presence of Him whom he believed, even God, who gives life to the dead and calls into being that which does not exist.*

18 *In hope against hope he believed, so that he might become a father of many nations according to that which had been spoken, "SO SHALL YOUR DESCENDANTS BE."*

19 *Without becoming weak in faith he contemplated his own body, now as good as dead since he was about a hundred years old, and the deadness of Sarah's womb;*

20 *yet, with respect to the promise of God, he did not waver in unbelief but grew strong in faith, giving glory to God,*

21 *and being fully assured that what God had promised, He was able also to perform.*

Week Six: **Love Doesn't . . .**

22 *Therefore IT WAS ALSO CREDITED TO HIM AS RIGHTEOUSNESS.*

23 *Now not for his sake only was it written that it was credited to him,*

24 *but for our sake also, to whom it will be credited, as those who believe in Him who raised Jesus our Lord from the dead,*

25 *He who was delivered over because of our transgressions, and was raised because of our justification.*

DISCUSS with your GROUP or PONDER on your own . . .

According to 1 Corinthians 13:5, love does not seek its own, is not provoked and does not take into account a wrong suffered. How can these three work together and influence one another?

Now, consider Romans 4. List everything your learned about "credited."

What did God do instead of counting Abraham's sin against him? On what basis?

What does God do today for those who believe?

Loving Like
JESUS
In a World that Hurts and Hates

How should people who do not have their sins counted against them treat those who sin against them?

OBSERVE the TEXT of SCRIPTURE

Let's take a look at what Paul says about sin accounting (again, the Greek *logizomai*) in 2 Corinthians 5.

READ 2 Corinthians 5:18-21 and **MARK** *counting*. Also **MARK** every word that has to do with *reconciliation.*

2 Corinthians 5:18-21

18 *Now all these things are from God, who reconciled us to Himself through Christ and gave us the ministry of reconciliation,*

19 *namely, that God was in Christ reconciling the world to Himself, not counting their trespasses against them, and He has committed to us the word of reconciliation.*

20 *Therefore, we are ambassadors for Christ, as though God were making an appeal through us; we beg you on behalf of Christ, be reconciled to God.*

21 *He made Him who knew no sin to be sin on our behalf, so that we might become the righteousness of God in Him.*

DISCUSS with your GROUP or PONDER on your own . . .

Make a list of what you learned about reconciliation. Who did the reconciling to start with? What effect did it have? What job do the reconciled now have?

How can you be an ambassador for Christ this week?

Loving Like
JESUS
In a World that Hurts and Hates

. . . REJOICE WITH UNRIGHTEOUSNESS

Paul tells his readers that love does not rejoice in unrighteousness (Greek: *adikia*). As we close our time of study this week, let's look at some other places where Paul talks about unrighteousness. As you'll notice in some of the following texts, *adikia* is also translated "wickedness."

ONE STEP FURTHER:

Blessed . . .

Not only don't Jesus' followers rejoice in unrighteousness, Jesus says they are blessed when they are *persecuted for the sake of righteousness:* if you have some extra time this week, check it out for yourself in Matthew 5:10-12. Also take a look at Acts 5:40-42. How can these words encourage you today?

OBSERVE the TEXT of SCRIPTURE

READ 1 Corinthians 13:6, Romans 1:18, 2 Thessalonians 2:8-12, and 2 Timothy 2:19 and **MARK** every reference to *unrighteousness* and *wickedness*. Then **MARK** every reference to *truth*.

1 Corinthians 13:6

6 *does not rejoice in unrighteousness, but rejoices with the truth;*

Romans 1:18

1 *For the wrath of God is revealed from heaven against all ungodliness and unrighteousness of men who suppress the truth in unrighteousness,*

2 Thessalonians 2:8-12

8 *Then that lawless one will be revealed whom the Lord will slay with the breath of His mouth and bring to an end by the appearance of His coming;*

9 *that is, the one whose coming is in accord with the activity of Satan, with all power and signs and false wonders,*

10 *and with all the deception of wickedness for those who perish, because they did not receive the love of the truth so as to be saved.*

11 *For this reason God will send upon them a deluding influence so that they will believe what is false,*

12 *in order that they all may be judged who did not believe the truth, but took pleasure in wickedness.*

2 Timothy 2:19

19 *Nevertheless, the firm foundation of God stands, having this seal, "The Lord knows those who are His," and, "Everyone who names the name of the Lord is to abstain from wickedness."*

DISCUSS with your GROUP or PONDER on your own . . .

What traits characterize the unrighteous/the wicked? How do they compare with the character of the righteous?

Loving Like
JESUS
In a World that Hurts and Hates

Based on these verses, how would you describe the interplay of truth and unrighteousness?

What implications do you think this is having on our society today?

@THE END OF THE DAY . . .

It's been a long week. Before you close your workbook, take some time to pray and to ask God to help you sort out what truth you most need to meditate on this week. Then, write it down below and be encouraged that it is God who is at work in you conforming you day by day to look more and more like Jesus.

Loving Like
JESUS
In a World that Hurts and Hates

Notes

Loving Like
JESUS
In a World that Hurts and Hates

Love Does . . .

" . . . bears all things, believes all things, hopes all things,
endures all things."
—1 Corinthians 13:7

Is love gullible? Does loving behavior involve something more or different from being the "doormat" of your family and social group? Does it blindly hope for a better tomorrow while rolling over belly-up during hard times?

Does it go "all-in" poker style no matter the circumstance? There's no denying that "all" is a very big little word and 1 Corinthians 13:7 is packed with it! Seriously, what do we do with this? Well, for starters we pay close attention to Inductive principles for interpretation! Let's get started.

Week Seven: **Love Does . . .**

REMEMBERING

Let's start off our time this week, remembering and reviewing what we've learned. I hope you'll write down not only the facts you've learned, but also with how God is using His truth to conform you more and more into the image of His son.

Love is . . .

Love isn't . . .

Love doesn't . . .

WHAT LOVE DOES . . .

. . . REJOICES WITH THE TRUTH

Last week we saw that "love does not rejoice in unrighteousness." Today we'll begin with the contrasting statement: "love rejoices with the truth." The phrase "rejoices with" in 1 Corinthians 13:6 comes from a single word in Greek: *sunchairo* (Greek: *sun*—with or together and *chairo*—rejoice). In order to help us better understand proper rejoicing with others, we'll look at two brief stories Jesus told in Luke 15.

OBSERVE the TEXT of SCRIPTURE

READ 1 Corinthians 13:6 and Luke 15:1-10. **MARK** *rejoice/rejoices*. In a distinctive way, also **MARK** *truth*.

1 Corinthians 13:6

  6 *does not rejoice in unrighteousness, but rejoices with the truth;*

Luke 15:1-10

1   Now all the tax collectors and the sinners were coming near Him to listen to Him.

2   Both the Pharisees and the scribes began to grumble, saying, "This man receives sinners and eats with them."

3   So He told them this parable, saying,

4   "What man among you, if he has a hundred sheep and has lost one of them, does not leave the ninety-nine in the open pasture and go after the one which is lost until he finds it?

5   "When he has found it, he lays it on his shoulders, rejoicing.

6   "And when he comes home, he calls together his friends and his neighbors, saying to them, 'Rejoice with me, for I have found my sheep which was lost!'

7   "I tell you that in the same way, there will be more joy in heaven over one sinner who repents than over ninety-nine righteous persons who need no repentance.

8   "Or what woman, if she has ten silver coins and loses one coin, does not light a lamp and sweep the house and search carefully until she finds it?

9   "When she has found it, she calls together her friends and neighbors, saying, 'Rejoice with me, for I have found the coin which I had lost!'

10   "In the same way, I tell you, there is joy in the presence of the angels of God over one sinner who repents."

DISCUSS with your GROUP or PONDER on your own . . .

Briefly summarize the two parables.

The Sheep:

The Coin:

What are the shepherd and the woman doing before the rejoicing starts? Why?

ONE STEP FURTHER:

Word Study: Rejoice

If you have some time this week, use your concordance to find where rejoice is used in Paul's writings and elsewhere in the New Testament. What do people rejoice over? What should they rejoice over? Is the Greek word used in other ways? If so, how? Record below what you learn.

Loving Like
JESUS
In a World that Hurts and Hates

Week Seven: **Love Does . . .**

What causes them to rejoice in each case?

ONE STEP FURTHER:

Word Study: *Sunchairo*

If you have some extra time this week, see how else *sunchairo* is used in the New Testament. Who rejoices with whom and why? Record what you find below.

Why does the joy spread?

How do each of the parables relate to sin or unrighteousness?

How does this relate to what we're learning in 1 Corinthians 13? What applications can we make?

OBSERVE the TEXT of SCRIPTURE

Before we move on, let's look at how all the members in a healthy functioning body respond to a single member in different circumstances.

READ 1 Corinthians 13:6 and Corinthians 12:24b-26 and **MARK** *rejoice/rejoices with.*

1 Corinthians 13:6

6 *does not rejoice in unrighteousness, but rejoices with the truth;*

1 Corinthians 12:24b-26

24 *But God has so composed the body, giving more abundant honor to that member which lacked,*

25 *so that there may be no division in the body, but that the members may have the same care for one another.*

26 And if one member suffers, all the members suffer with it; if one member is honored, all the members rejoice with it.

DISCUSS with your GROUP or PONDER on your own . . .

What should and should not characterize the body of believers?

What are proper responses to suffering and honor within the body? How do these fit the descriptions of love in 1 Corinthians 13:6?

Now, let's consider for a moment some *actual* Corinthian behavior reported "among" them in 1 Corinthians 5:1-2. How *did* they respond? How does Paul say the body *should have* responded?

As believers, do we ever ignore or even rejoice over things we should mourn over? What can we rejoice with or about? What things can we *not* rejoice with or about?

How can we remain loving when we cannot in good conscience "rejoice" with someone?

What challenges do we face in doing this?

ONE STEP FURTHER:

How Was Corinth Doing?
If you have some time this week, see what else you can learn about the behavior of the Corinthian church. How were they doing as a body? Although we've already looked at it, don't forget to include 1 Corinthians 5:1-2. How were the Corinthians behaving? How could they have done better? What can we learn from them? Record what you discover below.

Loving Like
JESUS
In a World that Hurts and Hates

Digging Deeper

Memorizing 1 Corinthians 13:4-7

Let's review!

Write 1 Corinthians 13:1-3 from memory. If you haven't memorized it word for word, write down the #hashtag version.

Here are a few different ways to think through and remember love's characteristics. You may have them grouped differently, but here are some groupings that have helped me.

Is/Isn't, Does/Doesn't Groupings

Love is: patient and kind

Love isn't: jealous, arrogant, provoked

Love does: rejoice (with truth), bear, believe, hope, endure

Love doesn't: brag, act unbecomingly, seek its own, account a wrong suffered, rejoice in unrighteousness

Related Characteristic Groupings

Because love is *kind,* it is *not jealous.*

Because love is *not arrogant,* it *does not brag.*

Because love *doesn't seek its own,* it *doesn't act unbecomingly.*

Because love *isn't provoked,* it *doesn't keep score (account a wrong suffered).*

Because love *rejoices in the truth,* it *doesn't rejoice in unrighteousness.*

Because love is *patient* and *kind* it always *bears, believes, hopes* and *endures.*

Is, Isn't, Does, Doesn't Patterns

v. 4	Two IS	Patient, Kind
	ISN'T, DOESN'T, ISN'T	Jealous, Brag, Arrogant
v. 5	Two DOESN'T	Act unbecomingly, Seek its own
	ISN'T, DOESN'T	Provoked, Account
v. 6	DOESN'T, DOES	Rejoice / Rejoice
v. 7	Four DOES	Bear, Believe, Hope, Endure

Digging Deeper

The Other Love Chapter: 1 John 4

If you have time this week, invest some of it in the other love chapter: 1 John 4. **MARK** love and then record what you learn about *love* from this text.

1 John 4:7-21

7 Beloved, let us love one another, for love is from God; and everyone who loves is born of God and knows God.

8 The one who does not love does not know God, for God is love.

9 By this the love of God was manifested in us, that God has sent His only begotten Son into the world so that we might live through Him.

10 In this is love, not that we loved God, but that He loved us and sent His Son to be the propitiation for our sins.

11 Beloved, if God so loved us, we also ought to love one another.

12 No one has seen God at any time; if we love one another, God abides in us, and His love is perfected in us.

13 By this we know that we abide in Him and He in us, because He has given us of His Spirit.

14 We have seen and testify that the Father has sent the Son to be the Savior of the world.

15 Whoever confesses that Jesus is the Son of God, God abides in him, and he in God.

16 We have come to know and have believed the love which God has for us. God is love, and the one who abides in love abides in God, and God abides in him.

17 By this, love is perfected with us, so that we may have confidence in the day of judgment; because as He is, so also are we in this world.

18 There is no fear in love; but perfect love casts out fear, because fear involves punishment, and the one who fears is not perfected in love.

19 We love, because He first loved us.

20 If someone says, "I love God," and hates his brother, he is a liar; for the one who does not love his brother whom he has seen, cannot love God whom he has not seen.

21 And this commandment we have from Him, that the one who loves God should love his brother also.

List what you learned about love from 1 John 4. (There's room to continue the list on the next page.)

Loving Like JESUS
In a World that Hurts and Hates

Week Seven: **Love Does . . .**

Here's a little more room for your "Love in 1 John 4" list.

How does John's teaching in 1 John support and complement Paul's teaching in 1 Corinthians 13?

What have you learned that you most need to apply? How will you begin doing that?

If you still have some extra time, find other passages in the Bible with love as a main theme and record them below along with your major takeaways from reading them.

LOVE and ALL THINGS . . .

One of the most known, quoted, and eloquent (at least in English!) verses of Scripture—"[love] bears all things, believes all things, hopes all things, endures all things"—is also one of the more misinterpreted. Before we jump in, let's review the basic inductive principles of interpretation that will prove particularly important as we look at this verse:

- Context rules

- Scripture is the best commentary on Scripture

- Scripture will never contradict Scripture

- Clear teaching helps us understand unclear teaching

- Interpret Scripture literally, taking into account literary genres

- Look for a single meaning

REASON THROUGH THE INTERPRETIVE PROBLEM

One issue at hand is in the phrase "believes all things." Taking it strictly at face value, what do you think this means? Go ahead and list as many possible meanings as you can think of.

Now, what misapplications could each lead to?

What about the other "all things"? What misinterpretations and misapplications easily jump out of this phrase, given the breadth of the English word "all"?

Loving Like
JESUS
In a World that Hurts and Hates

Stick with me here. Since this verse has such opportunity for misinterpretation, it's critical that we do our interpretive duty of cross-referencing to rule out errant interpretations and to home in on the most likely interpretations.

We'll start by looking at some scriptures that will help us discover what phrases in this text *can't* mean. To do this most efficiently, we're going to start by looking at "[love] believes all things." Jesus Himself helps us rule some things out quite quickly. Let's take a look . . .

BELIEVES ALL

If you think Christians should live gullible, doe-eyed lives, think again!

OBSERVE the TEXT of SCRIPTURE

READ Matthew 24:1-28 and **MARK** the phrase *do not believe* and any synonymous phrases.

Matthew 24:1-28

1 *Jesus came out from the temple and was going away when His disciples came up to point out the temple buildings to Him.*

2 *And He said to them, "Do you not see all these things? Truly I say to you, not one stone here will be left upon another, which will not be torn down."*

3 *As He was sitting on the Mount of Olives, the disciples came to Him privately, saying, "Tell us, when will these things happen, and what will be the sign of Your coming, and of the end of the age?"*

4 *And Jesus answered and said to them, "See to it that no one misleads you.*

5 *"For many will come in My name, saying, 'I am the Christ,' and will mislead many.*

6 *"You will be hearing of wars and rumors of wars. See that you are not frightened, for those things must take place, but that is not yet the end.*

7 *"For nation will rise against nation, and kingdom against kingdom, and in various places there will be famines and earthquakes.*

8 *"But all these things are merely the beginning of birth pangs.*

9 *"Then they will deliver you to tribulation, and will kill you, and you will be hated by all nations because of My name.*

10 *"At that time many will fall away and will betray one another and hate one another.*

11 *"Many false prophets will arise and will mislead many.*

12 *"Because lawlessness is increased, most people's love will grow cold.*

13 *"But the one who endures to the end, he will be saved.*

14 *"This gospel of the kingdom shall be preached in the whole world as a testimony to all the nations, and then the end will come.*

15 "Therefore when you see the ABOMINATION OF DESOLATION which was spoken of through Daniel the prophet, standing in the holy place (let the reader understand),

16 then those who are in Judea must flee to the mountains.

17 "Whoever is on the housetop must not go down to get the things out that are in his house.

18 "Whoever is in the field must not turn back to get his cloak.

19 "But woe to those who are pregnant and to those who are nursing babies in those days!

20 "But pray that your flight will not be in the winter, or on a Sabbath.

21 "For then there will be a great tribulation, such as has not occurred since the beginning of the world until now, nor ever will.

22 "Unless those days had been cut short, no life would have been saved; but for the sake of the elect those days will be cut short.

23 "Then if anyone says to you, 'Behold, here is the Christ,' or 'There He is,' do not believe him.

24 "For false Christs and false prophets will arise and will show great signs and wonders, so as to mislead, if possible, even the elect.

25 "Behold, I have told you in advance.

26 "So if they say to you, 'Behold, He is in the wilderness,' do not go out, or, 'Behold, He is in the inner rooms,' do not believe them.

27 "For just as the lightning comes from the east and flashes even to the west, so will the coming of the Son of Man be.

28 "Wherever the corpse is, there the vultures will gather.

DISCUSS with your GROUP or PONDER on your own . . .

Describe the setting of this passage. What question is Jesus responding to?

What does Jesus warn about beginning in verse 4? How often does He repeat this warning and with what other phrasing?

ONE STEP FURTHER:

More "Do Not Believe"s

If you have some extra time, check out what John writes in 1 John 1:1-6 about what to believe and what not to believe. Compare what he says with Jesus' teaching in Matthew 24 and record your observations below.

Loving Like
JESUS
In a World that Hurts and Hates

Week Seven: **Love Does . . .**

While we're here, according to verses 11 and 12 what will arise and what will increase during this time?

How will this phenomenon affect most people's love?

Have you noticed it having this effect on you? If so, in what ways?

How can you guard against this chilling property?

What specifically does Jesus say *not to* believe in verses 23–26? Why?

Given this, what meaning can we rule out for "love believes all things" in 1 Corinthians 13:7? Why?

OBSERVE the TEXT of SCRIPTURE

While context shows us that Jesus was speaking to the twelve disciples He was sending out, His teaching is applicable to disciples today.

READ Matthew 10:16-22 and **UNDERLINE** everything Jesus commands.

Matthew 10:16-22

16 *"Behold, I send you out as sheep in the midst of wolves; so be shrewd as serpents and innocent as doves.*

17 *"But beware of men, for they will hand you over to the courts and scourge you in their synagogues;*

18 *and you will even be brought before governors and kings for My sake, as a testimony to them and to the Gentiles.*

19 *"But when they hand you over, do not worry about how or what you are to say; for it will be given you in that hour what you are to say.*

20 *"For it is not you who speak, but it is the Spirit of your Father who speaks in you.*

21 *"Brother will betray brother to death, and a father his child; and children will rise up against parents and cause them to be put to death.*

22 *"You will be hated by all because of My name, but it is the one who has endured to the end who will be saved.*

DISCUSS with your GROUP or PONDER on your own . . .

How does Jesus describe the situation He is sending His disciples into? What does this say about the disciples? About the world?

What does this situation necessitate on behalf of the "sheep"? What precautions will they need to take and why?

What specifics does Jesus warn about? What will the wolves do?

FYI:

Text Comparisons

Here are some different ways translators have read 1 Corinthians 13:7.

NASB

"[Love] bears all things, believes all things, hopes all things, endures all things."

ESV

"Love bears all things, believes all things, hopes all things, endures all things."

NKJV

"[Love] bears all things, believes all things, hopes all things, endures all things."

NIV

"It always protects, always trusts, always hopes, always perseveres."

NLT

"Love never gives up, never loses faith, is always hopeful, and endures through every circumstance."

Loving Like
JESUS
In a World that Hurts and Hates

Week Seven: **Love Does . . .**

What provisions has Jesus made for the sheep?

What will He accomplish?

How can being "shrewd as serpents" and "innocent as doves" help navigating in a hating, wolfish world?

How does this passage fit with "[love] believes all things"?

HOW DO WE TRANSLATE THE GREEK *TA PANTA?*

A repeated term in 1 Corinthians 13:7 hits like a ton of bricks: four times Paul says "all things." That's how the scholars of the three major versions (the KJV, NASB, and the ESV) consistently translated it. Because there's obviously some relativity intrinsic to "all," a few paraphrase editions (see the bottom 2 in the margin of the previous page) suggest changing this phrase from an adjective/noun to an adverb—from "believes all things" to "always believes." A simple inductive study of *panta* (the accusative neuter plural of the adjective *pas* ["all"] shows that while it is in fact an adjective it does not mean universally all things. Disciples who live as innocent as doves and as wise as serpents can believe "all things" God reveals (the "all knowledge" specified in Romans 15:14; 1 Corinthians 1:5; 13:2; see also Luke 24:44; Acts 2:18, 24; 10:43) without believing everything man says!

OBSERVE the TEXT of SCRIPTURE

As 1 Corinthians 13 gives us a 3-D look at love, Hebrews 11 does the same for faith. In this chapter you'll see how "believes all things" is qualified in biblical history.

READ 1 Corinthians 13:7 and **MARK** *believes.* Then, **READ** Hebrews 11 in your Bible and pay attention to the word "faith" (Greek: *pistis*), the noun form of the verb "believe" (Greek: *pisteuo*). If you write in your Bible, take the time to **MARK** *faith* throughout Hebrews 11.

1 Corinthians 13:7

7 [Love] bears all things, believes all things, hopes all things, endures all things.

DISCUSS with your GROUP or PONDER on your own . . .

Briefly describe faith as portrayed in Hebrews 11.

How do the champions of faith in Hebrews 11 illustrate love's connection to bearing, believing, hoping, and enduring (1 Corinthians 13:7)?

BEARS ALL

The Greek word translated "bears" in 1 Corinthians 13:7 is *stego* which also means "to cover." The word "roof" comes from the same Greek root (see, e.g., Luke 7:6). Let's look at how Paul uses the word in 1 Corinthians 9:12 where it is translated "endures." We'll also look at a cross-reference in 1 Peter where a different Greek word (*kaleptei*) is used, but a similar meaning seems to be in play.

OBSERVE the TEXT of SCRIPTURE

READ 1 Corinthians 9:1-12 and **MARK** *endure*. **UNDERLINE** everything Paul and Barnabas have a "right" to.

1 Corinthians 9:1-12

1 Am I not free? Am I not an apostle? Have I not seen Jesus our Lord? Are you not my work in the Lord?

2 If to others I am not an apostle, at least I am to you; for you are the seal of my apostleship in the Lord.

3 My defense to those who examine me is this:

4 Do we not have a right to eat and drink?

5 Do we not have a right to take along a believing wife, even as the rest of the apostles and the brothers of the Lord and Cephas?

FYI:

Bearing and Overlooking
A man's discretion makes him slow to anger, and it is his glory to overlook a transgression.

—Proverbs 19:11

Loving Like
JESUS
In a World that Hurts and Hates

6   *Or do only Barnabas and I not have a right to refrain from working?*

7   *Who at any time serves as a soldier at his own expense? Who plants a vineyard and does not eat the fruit of it? Or who tends a flock and does not use the milk of the flock?*

8   *I am not speaking these things according to human judgment, am I? Or does not the Law also say these things?*

9   *For it is written in the Law of Moses, "You shall not muzzle the ox while he is threshing." God is not concerned about oxen, is He?*

10   *Or is He speaking altogether for our sake? Yes, for our sake it was written, because the plowman ought to plow in hope, and the thresher to thresh in hope of sharing the crops.*

11   *If we sowed spiritual things in you, is it too much if we reap material things from you?*

12   *If others share the right over you, do we not more? Nevertheless, we did not use this right, but we endure all things so that we will cause no hindrance to the gospel of Christ.*

READ 1 Peter 4:8 and **MARK** *covers.*

1 Peter 4:8

8   *Above all, keep fervent in your love for one another, because love covers a multitude of sins.*

DISCUSS with your GROUP or PONDER on your own . . .

What rights did Paul and Barnabas forgo for the Corinthians?

Why did they "endure" or "bear" all the Corinthians' issues? Why do you think they were able to bear them? What was more important to Paul and Barnabas?

How might Peter's exhortation tie in with this?

How are you at bearing with people instead of calling out every violation? Just asking.

HOPES AND ENDURES ALL

Let's look at the final two together.

OBSERVE the TEXT of SCRIPTURE

READ Romans 8:18-25 and **MARK** *hope* and *perseverance* (Greek: *hupomone*).

Romans 8:18-25

18 *For I consider that the sufferings of this present time are not worthy to be compared with the glory that is to be revealed to us.*

19 *For the anxious longing of the creation waits eagerly for the revealing of the sons of God.*

20 *For the creation was subjected to futility, not willingly, but because of Him who subjected it, in hope*

21 *that the creation itself also will be set free from its slavery to corruption into the freedom of the glory of the children of God.*

22 *For we know that the whole creation groans and suffers the pains of childbirth together until now.*

23 *And not only this, but also we ourselves, having the first fruits of the Spirit, even we ourselves groan within ourselves, waiting eagerly for our adoption as sons, the redemption of our body.*

24 *For in hope we have been saved, but hope that is seen is not hope; for who hopes for what he already sees?*

25 *But if we hope for what we do not see, with perseverance we wait eagerly for it.*

> **FYI:**
>
> **Complete, Nothing Lacking**
> *Consider it all joy, my brethren, when you encounter various trials, knowing that the testing of your faith produces endurance. And let endurance have its perfect result, so that you may be perfect and complete, lacking in nothing.*
>
> —James 1:2-4

DISCUSS with your GROUP or PONDER on your own . . .

List everything this passage says about hope.

Loving Like
JESUS
In a World that Hurts and Hates

How can hope be both unseen and fully reliable?

How does "love hopes all things" (1 Corinthians 13:7) show up in actions?

ONE STEP FURTHER:

Word Study: Endures

If you have time to pick one word study for this whole class, pick this one. See what you can learn about *hupomone* (noun) and *hupomeno* (verb), respective Greek words for "endurance" and "endure." Where are they used in the New Testament? What roots make up these compound Greek words? What is *hupomone* and how do we get it? Get digging, have fun, and record what you discover below!

OBSERVE the TEXT of SCRIPTURE

READ Romans 5:1-11 and again **MARK** *hope* and *perserverance (hupomone)*. Then go back and **MARK** every reference to *love*.

Romans 5:1-11

1   Therefore, having been justified by faith, we have peace with God through our Lord Jesus Christ,

2   through whom also we have obtained our introduction by faith into this grace in which we stand; and we exult in hope of the glory of God.

3   And not only this, but we also exult in our tribulations, knowing that tribulation brings about perseverance;

4   and perseverance, proven character; and proven character, hope;

5   and hope does not disappoint, because the love of God has been poured out within our hearts through the Holy Spirit who was given to us.

6   For while we were still helpless, at the right time Christ died for the ungodly.

7   For one will hardly die for a righteous man; though perhaps for the good man someone would dare even to die.

8   But God demonstrates His own love toward us, in that while we were yet sinners, Christ died for us.

9   Much more then, having now been justified by His blood, we shall be saved from the wrath of God through Him.

10 For if while we were enemies we were reconciled to God through the death of His Son, much more, having been reconciled, we shall be saved by His life.

11 And not only this, but we also exult in God through our Lord Jesus Christ, through whom we have now received the reconciliation.

DISCUSS with your GROUP or PONDER on your own . . .

According to Romans 5 what produces endurance or perseverance? What do you think of this? Why?

What relationship does perseverance have to hope?

What is the hope in "hope"? Why can we count on it? Why will it not disappoint?

According to Romans 5:5 how can you and I love in 1 Corinthians 13 ways?

When did God love us? How can this truth help us love those who hurt and hate?

@THE END OF THE DAY . . .

Take some time to pray and to think back through everything we've covered this week. Then write down the most important truth you need to remember and put into action.

Week Seven: **Love Does . . .**

Week Eight

Love Remains

"But now faith, hope, love, abide these three; but the greatest of these is love."
—1 Corinthians 13:13

We've traveled many miles these past few weeks covering just seven verses of Scripture, studying deeply and turning the gem slowly to appreciate the intricacies of its beauty and the implications of truth. This final week we're going to pick up the pace as we look at 1 Corinthians 13:8-13. I know, it's not exactly light speed, but compared to what we've been doing we'll be pretty close to flying!

Week Eight: **Love Remains**

REMEMBERING

Let's take a few minutes to review where we've been.

Love is . . .

Love isn't . . .

Love doesn't . . .

Love does . . .

How has what you've learned about love been changing the way you think and act?

SOME THINGS WILL BE DONE AWAY WITH . . .

Before we finish our time in 1 Corinthians 13, we have one more murky theological river to cross. Put on your waders, we're going in!

OBSERVE the TEXT of SCRIPTURE

READ 1 Corinthians 13:8-13 and **CIRCLE** any references to spiritual gifts. **MARK** the phrase *done away* and any synonyms.

1 Corinthians 13:8-13

8   *Love never fails; but if there are gifts of prophecy, they will be done away; if there are tongues, they will cease; if there is knowledge, it will be done away.*

9   *For we know in part and we prophesy in part;*

10 *but when the perfect comes, the partial will be done away.*

11 *When I was a child, I used to speak like a child, think like a child, reason like a child; when I became a man, I did away with childish things.*

12 *For now we see in a mirror dimly, but then face to face; now I know in part, but then I will know fully just as I also have been fully known.*

13 *But now faith, hope, love, abide these three; but the greatest of these is love.*

DISCUSS with your GROUP or PONDER on your own . . .

What spiritual gifts does Paul reference in this section?

What does Paul say will be "done away"?

What question does that leave us with?

**Loving Like
JESUS**
In a World that Hurts and Hates

Digging Deeper

Memorizing 1 Corinthians 13:8-13

Let's review!

1 Corinthians 13:1-3

Write 1 Corinthians 13:1-3 from memory. If you haven't memorized it word for word, write down the #hashtag version.

1 Corinthians 13:4-7

Write 1 Corinthians 13:4-7 from memory. Again, if you haven't memorized it word for word, write down the #hashtag version.

1 Corinthians 13:8-13

First Corinthians 13:8-13 has an "If" / "Then"; "Partial" / "Perfect"; "Child" / "Man";
"Now" / "Then"pattern that is helpful to watch when memorizing. See if this helps, then in
the space at the bottom of the page note any other patterns or memory hooks that *you* see.

If	**Then**
if there are gifts of prophecy	they will be done away
if there are tongues	they will cease
if there is knowledge	it will be done away

Partial	**Perfect**
we know in part	the partial will be done away
we prophesy in part	

Child	**Man**
used to speak like a child	did away with childish things
think like a child	
reason like a child	

Now	**Then**
we see in a mirror dimly	[we will see] face to face
I know in part	I will know fully

These Abide

Faith

Hope

Love

Notes

THE PARTIAL WON'T LAST . . .

Let's mark some different words in the next section to see if we can answer the question: *When will prophecy, knowledge, and tongues be "done away"?*

OBSERVE the TEXT of SCRIPTURE

READ 1 Corinthians 13:8-13 and **MARK** the phrase *in part* and any synonyms (*child, dimly,* etc.). Also **MARK** *perfect* and any synonyms (*man, face to face,* etc.) in a distinctive way.

1 Corinthians 13:8-13

8 *Love never fails; but if there are gifts of prophecy, they will be done away; if there are tongues, they will cease; if there is knowledge, it will be done away.*

9 *For we know in part and we prophesy in part;*

10 *but when the perfect comes, the partial will be done away.*

11 *When I was a child, I used to speak like a child, think like a child, reason like a child; when I became a man, I did away with childish things.*

12 *For now we see in a mirror dimly, but then face to face; now I know in part, but then I will know fully just as I also have been fully known.*

13 *But now faith, hope, love, abide these three; but the greatest of these is love.*

DISCUSS with your GROUP or PONDER on your own . . .

What does Paul describe as being partial in verse 9?

What other metaphors or situations does he use to describe "partial"?

How does Paul describe "the perfect"?

. . . WHEN THE PERFECT COMES

Paul clearly says that the partial will be done away when the perfect comes, but we're still left with the question of what he means by "when the perfect comes." Let's see if asking some more inductive questions will help shed some light.

OBSERVE the TEXT of SCRIPTURE

READ 1 Corinthians 13:8-13 and **MARK** any references to time (*never, when, now, then*, etc.).

1 Corinthians 13:8-13

8 *Love never fails; but if there are gifts of prophecy, they will be done away; if there are tongues, they will cease; if there is knowledge, it will be done away.*

9 *For we know in part and we prophesy in part;*

10 *but when the perfect comes, the partial will be done away.*

11 *When I was a child, I used to speak like a child, think like a child, reason like a child; when I became a man, I did away with childish things.*

12 *For now we see in a mirror dimly, but then face to face; now I know in part, but then I will know fully just as I also have been fully known.*

13 *But now faith, hope, love, abide these three; but the greatest of these is love.*

DISCUSS with your GROUP or PONDER on your own . . .

How does Paul describe his "now"?

Based on the "time" words you examined, was Paul living during the time of the partial or the perfect? Explain.

According to verse 10, when will the partial be done away? Again, what gifts does Paul specifically define as "partial"?

ONE STEP FURTHER:

Word Study: Perfect

If you have a little more time, find the Greek word translated "perfect" in 1 Corinthians 13:10. See how it's translated in Paul's writings and elsewhere in the New Testament. Does this help you understand what Paul means here? Record what you learn below.

Loving Like
JESUS
In a World that Hurts and Hates

Week Eight: **Love Remains**

When Paul uses "then" two times in verse 12, what is he talking about, the partial or the perfect?

Do you think "the perfect" has come yet? Why/why not?

. . . BUT LOVE ENDURES FOREVER

While we may come to different conclusions on "when the perfect" will come, Paul is clear that love will never fail!

OBSERVE the TEXT of SCRIPTURE

READ 1 Corinthians 13:8-13 and **MARK** any references to *love*.

1 Corinthians 13:8-13

8 *Love never fails; but if* there are gifts of *prophecy, they will be done away; if* there are *tongues, they will cease; if* there is *knowledge, it will be done away.*

9 *For we know in part and we prophesy in part;*

10 *but when the perfect comes, the partial will be done away.*

11 *When I was a child, I used to speak like a child, think like a child, reason like a child; when I became a man, I did away with childish things.*

12 *For now we see in a mirror dimly, but then face to face; now I know in part, but then I will know fully just as I also have been fully known.*

13 *But now faith, hope, love, abide these three; but the greatest of these is love.*

DISCUSS with your GROUP or PONDER on your own . . .

According to this passage, what does love do? What does it *not* do?

FYI:

Love Never Fails

The Greek word *pipto* that Paul uses in verse 8 is translated "fails." Elsewhere in the New Testament it is almost exclusively translated as a form of "fall." "Falls" and "falters" may be related in old English and here the negated word contrasts the permanence of love against the ephemeral nature of gifts. In the face of hardship and trial, love never fails. Love has never failed. Love will never fail. Love abides.

Loving Like
JESUS
In a World that Hurts and Hates

How does love compare with the spiritual gifts mentioned?

How does love compare with faith and hope?

Let's just say, for a second, that you're getting fussy over whether or not certain spiritual gifts have ceased and what other people think about it. Based on this chapter, how do you think you should respond?

THE GREATEST COMMANDMENT

When a Pharisee asks Jesus what the greatest commandment is, He refers the man back to Deuteronomy.

OBSERVE the TEXT of SCRIPTURE

READ Matthew 22:36-40 and **MARK** any references to *love*.

Matthew 22:36-40

36 *"Teacher, which is the great commandment in the Law?"*

37 *And He said to him, " 'YOU SHALL LOVE THE LORD YOUR GOD WITH ALL YOUR HEART, AND WITH ALL YOUR SOUL, AND WITH ALL YOUR MIND.'*

38 *"This is the great and foremost commandment.*

39 *"The second is like it, 'YOU SHALL LOVE YOUR NEIGHBOR AS YOURSELF.'*

40 *On these two commandments depend the whole Law and the Prophets."*

DISCUSS with your GROUP or PONDER on your own . . .

What does Jesus say is the greatest commandment?

FYI:

Deuteronomy 6:4-9
"Hear, O Israel! The LORD is our God, the LORD is one! You shall love the LORD your God with all your heart and with all your soul and with all your might. These words, which I am commanding you today, shall be on your heart. You shall teach them diligently to your sons and shall talk of them when you sit in your house and when you walk by the way and when you lie down and when you rise up. You shall bind them as a sign on your hand and they shall be as frontals on your forehead. You shall write them on the doorposts of your house and on your gates."

Loving Like
JESUS
In a World that Hurts and Hates

What does this involve practically? What do you think is another way of saying "all of your heart, and with all of your soul, and with all of your mind"?

ONE STEP FURTHER:

What God Looks For

If you have time this week, read the account of King Asa in 2 Chronicles 16. Record what you learn below, paying close attention to verse 9.

How are you doing at this?

Why do you think Jesus answered with more than one commandment?

What was the second part of His answer?

How do the whole Law and the Prophets depend on these?

How are you doing at the second part?

Loving Like
JESUS
In a World that Hurts and Hates

What are your biggest remaining challenges? Why do you think these challenges are hanging around? What is your next step?

BUT I SAY TO YOU

The greatest commandment was clear enough but Jesus ups the ante by extending the love command to enemies during His famous teaching often referred to as the Sermon on the Mount.

OBSERVE the TEXT of SCRIPTURE

READ Matthew 5:43-48 and **MARK** any references to *love*.

Matthew 5:43-48

43 *"You have heard that it was said, 'YOU SHALL LOVE YOUR NEIGHBOR and hate your enemy.'*

44 *"But I say to you, love your enemies and pray for those who persecute you,*

45 *so that you may be sons of your Father who is in heaven; for He causes His sun to rise on the evil and the good, and sends rain on the righteous and the unrighteous.*

46 *"For if you love those who love you, what reward do you have? Do not even the tax collectors do the same?*

47 *"If you greet only your brothers, what more are you doing than others? Do not even the Gentiles do the same?*

48 *"Therefore you are to be perfect, as your heavenly Father is perfect.*

DISCUSS with your GROUP or PONDER on your own . . .

Where had the Jewish people heard "You shall love your neighbor"?

Where do you think they heard the second part of the statement "and hate your enemy"?

How do most people respond toward enemies? How does Jesus stand this on its head? How does He say to treat enemies?

FYI:

Love Your Neighbor

God commands His people to love their neighbors, but He says nothing about hating their enemies—that came from somewhere else!

"You shall not take vengeance, nor bear any grudge against the sons of your people, but you shall love your neighbor as yourself; I am the LORD."

—Leviticus 19:18

Loving Like
JESUS
In a World that Hurts and Hates

Week Eight: **Love Remains**

So we're clear, what behavior might be attributed to enemies just from this passage of Scripture?

What kind of behavior distinguishes Christian love from secular definitions of love?

Why are Christians to love this way? How *can* they love this way?

FRUIT OF THE SPIRIT . . . .

The flesh and the Spirit war against each other and the actions and outcome of walking according to each are visible.

OBSERVE the TEXT of SCRIPTURE

READ Galatians 5:16-26 and **MARK** any references to *the Spirit*.

Galatians 5:16-26

16 But I say, walk by the Spirit, and you will not carry out the desire of the flesh.

17 For the flesh sets its desire against the Spirit, and the Spirit against the flesh; for these are in opposition to one another, so that you may not do the things that you please.

18 But if you are led by the Spirit, you are not under the Law.

19 Now the deeds of the flesh are evident, which are: immorality, impurity, sensuality,

20 idolatry, sorcery, enmities, strife, jealousy, outbursts of anger, disputes, dissensions, factions,

Loving Like
JESUS
In a World that Hurts and Hates

21 *envying, drunkenness, carousing, and things like these, of which I forewarn you, just as I have forewarned you, that those who practice such things will not inherit the kingdom of God.*

22 *But the fruit of the Spirit is love, joy, peace, patience, kindness, goodness, faithfulness,*

23 *gentleness, self-control; against such things there is no law.*

24 *Now those who belong to Christ Jesus have crucified the flesh with its passions and desires.*

25 *If we live by the Spirit, let us also walk by the Spirit.*

26 *Let us not become boastful, challenging one another, envying one another.*

DISCUSS with your GROUP or PONDER on your own . . .

List what the text says about the Spirit.

Conversely, what are the deeds of the flesh and what does Paul say about them?

Are any of these deeds of the flesh things that love isn't or doesn't? Explain.

What is the core of Paul's warning regarding the deeds of the flesh?

How does Paul describe the fruit of the Spirit?

FYI:

The Power to Obey

I have been crucified with Christ; and it is no longer I who live, but Christ lives in me; and the life which I now live in the flesh I live by faith in the Son of God, who loved me and gave Himself up for me.

—Galatians 2:20

Loving Like
JESUS
In a World that Hurts and Hates

Week Eight: **Love Remains**

What does Paul say is true of those who belong to Jesus?

What does "crucified the flesh" mean? What will this involve in your life?

How are those who live by the Spirit to walk?

How do the truths of Galatians 5 compliment what we've studied in 1 Corinthians 13?

@THE END OF THE DAY . . .

Take some time to pray and review what we've learned this week and over the course of our time together. Then, jot down the most important thing or things you need to remember. Remember, sometimes less is more. When you've finished this, take a few more minutes to consider what your next step in Bible study will be . . . maybe it's time to take what you've learned in this study to others!

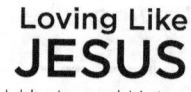

Loving Like
JESUS
In a World that Hurts and Hates

So, where do we go from here? We've been wrestling with how to live this out in a world that is combative, in a world that is difficult. My challenge to you, and to myself, is to pay attention to others out there who also lean in toward truth – maybe they think a little differently than you on some things, or are of a different age, or come from different circumstances, but their hearts are inclined toward truth -- lean into those people and start building bridges across generations, across races, start listening and start a dialogue that's based on the Word of God. If we can seek to live in love, to walk in love, to actively engage others who are also leaning in -- if we can find unity in Christ, a unity that Jesus talks about, what a witness that will be to the world!

I want to thank you for being with me on this journey. I pray that we will go forth and continue to love one another like Jesus.

Pam

Learn more

Find more books, studies and resources at

www.pamgillaspie.com

Connect with others

Be an ambassador, FOLLOW, LIKE and SHARE us with your social network.

 pamgillaspie

 pamgillaspie

Loving Like
JESUS
In a World that Hurts and Hates

RESOURCES

Helpful Study Tools

The New How to Study Your Bible
Eugene, Oregon: Harvest House
Publishers

The New Inductive Study Bible
Eugene, Oregon: Harvest House
Publishers

Logos Bible Software
Available at www.logos.com.

Greek Word Study Tools

Kittel, G., Friedrich, G., & Bromiley,
G.W.
*Theological Dictionary of the New
Testament, Abridged* (also known as
Little Kittel)
Grand Rapids, Michigan: W.B.
Eerdmans Publishing Company

Zodhiates, Spiros
*The Complete Word Study Dictionary:
New Testament*
Chattanooga, Tennessee: AMG
Publishers

Hebrew Word Study Tools

Harris, R.L., Archer, G.L., & Walker,
B.K.
*Theological Wordbook of the Old
Testament* (also known as TWOT)
Chicago, Illinois: Moody Press

Zodhiates, Spiros
*The Complete Word Study Dictionary:
Old Testament*
Chattanooga, Tennessee: AMG
Publishers

General Word Study Tools

Strong, James
*The New Strong's Exhaustive
Concordance of the Bible*
Nashville, Tennessee: Thomas Nelson

Recommended Commentary Sets

Expositor's Bible Commentary
Grand Rapids, Michigan: Zondervan

NIV Application Commentary
Grand Rapids, Michigan: Zondervan

The New American Commentary
Nashville, Tennessee: Broadman and
Holman Publishers

One-Volume Commentaries

Carson, D.A., France, R.T., Motyer,
J.A., & Wenham, G.J. Ed.
*New Bible Commentary: 21st Century
Edition*
Downers Grove, Illinois: Inter-Varsity
Press

Rydelnik, M.,.Vanlaningham, M., Ed.
The Moody Bible Commentary
Chicago, Illinois: Moody Publishers

Loving Like
JESUS
In a World that Hurts and Hates